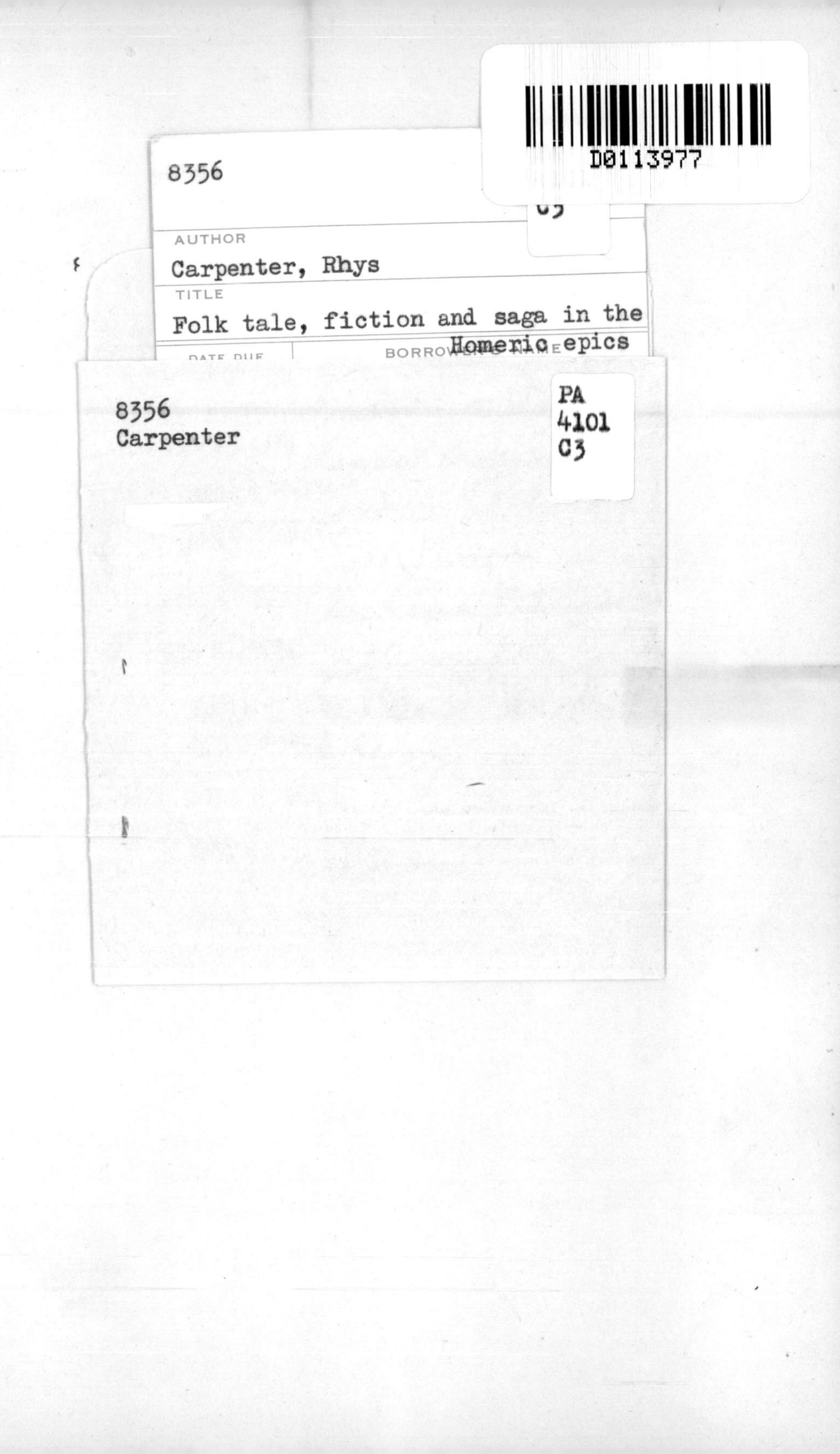

SATHER CLASSICAL LECTURES

VOLUME TWENTY

FOLK TALE, FICTION, AND SAGA IN THE HOMERIC EPICS

FOLK TALE, FICTION AND SAGA IN THE HOMERIC EPICS

BY

RHYS CARPENTER

UNIVERSITY OF CALIFORNIA PRESS
BERKELEY AND LOS ANGELES
1956

UNIVERSITY OF CALIFORNIA PRESS
BERKELEY AND LOS ANGELES
CALIFORNIA

◇

CAMBRIDGE UNIVERSITY PRESS
LONDON, ENGLAND

Second printing, 1956

MANUFACTURED IN THE UNITED STATES OF AMERICA

TO

B. B.

LAST OF THE ARKEISIAN CLAN

FOR TRUE FRIENDSHIP'S SAKE

CONTENTS

CHAPTER I

LITERATURE WITHOUT LETTERS

THE STUDY of literature is an enterprise so vast that no one human mind can cope with it successfully. The multiplicity of languages, the centuries of time, are too formidable. Books and manuscripts, printed or written, recent, medieval, and ancient, make a total too great for a single lifetime's reading. And yet this terrifying array, stretching from the pyramid texts of Egypt down to the novels of our own day, derives from only a fraction of the years and a portion of the lands in which human literary activity has flourished—if we will admit the etymological contradiction that literature may exist without letters.

The craft of printing is only five hundred years old; European knowledge of paper dates back only a thousand years; the very art of writing has been known to most European peoples for less than two thousand years and nowhere, not even in China or Egypt or Mesopotamia, seems to be appreciably older than five thousand. A respectable antiquity, this last one! But how much older still are poetry and song and the craft of telling enthralling stories to attentive ears? Without benefit of writing, songs may be composed, sung, remembered, and sung again; adventures may be told, incidents, anecdotes, and marvelous happenings recounted; even poetry of great range and power and beauty may come into being and persist, nor die with the passing of its maker. Beside and beyond the known realm of written literature stretches interminably the almost unknown world of oral literature, whose merest fraction has been reduced to written or printed form.

Speech must be almost as old as humankind; song must be almost as old as speech; and poetry almost as old as song. Against this enormous vista, writing, on which our normal literary types depend, is almost a modernism. It is idle to ask how old is language, since no one, seemingly, yet knows securely the age of sentient loquent man; wherefore it is impossible to venture even a plausible guess at the antiquity of oral literary forms. Yet it is fairly safe to say that, with the antiquity of writing nowhere transcending five thousand years, the literature of unwritten speech must outdate its written competitor and successor by many times its measure. Attic tragedy and history, Plato and the pre-Socratics, will then become milestones set only a little distance back along the road which leads to the shadowy unwritten beginnings of literature. What seems a giant stride back into the past from Ibsen to Aeschylos is but a step that could be repeated many times before we should come to man's primal discovery of the magic of assonances and cadences, when he began to use speech for something more than the mere grunted communication of his immediate want. But these other steps behind Aeschylos are steps into darkness where it is difficult to catch even a glimmer of a lost world.

Yet we are not, like the paleontologists, seeking for things utterly extinct. Out of this immeasurable past, oral literature still survives today, both in its own right in its own true oral forms as well as in written record of itself, preserved before it died out in the past. But it has suffered and diminished greatly, and in many lands where once it flourished it is all but extinct today, because literacy, the spreading use of writing, everywhere sooner or later destroys it.

Perhaps you remember the scene in Victor Hugo's *Notre-Dame* where a cleric makes the rather cryptic remark that the printed book will ultimately destroy the carven edifice of the cathedral wherein architecture and its attendant arts in the past had set the visual record of man's thoughts. "The book will kill the building," he insists; "this will kill that—*ceci tuera cela!*"

So it has been with the impact of writing on oral literature:

"ceci tuera cela!" And human memory, which once perforce kept all human records, relinquished its powers to the newcomer and grew proportionately enfeebled with this cession of her strength. Most of us today can hardly credit the achievement of the *illiterati* who knew the Koran by heart or carried the entire Iliad and Odyssey in their minds. But nowadays whoever trusts his library and notebooks may no longer trust his remembrance. Only where memory cannot be displaced, as in the concert recitals of musicians or the operatic roles of singers, can we still observe its prodigious powers. But originally Mnemosyne was mother of *all* the Muses.

In the world of today, where the spread of literacy has remorselessly been destroying the oral literary forms and only the lowest cultural levels preserve their preliterate traditions, oral literature has had to take refuge with the peasant and with backward cultures. But there the strata which have escaped schooling will continue to foster it, and in all levels the children still too young to have acquired letters will be its eager audience. But the mature, the intelligent, the gifted of mankind will despise and neglect it and let it die. For this reason it has been able to survive only in such forms as the peasant or the immature mind likes, understands, and practices. Yet it has not always been so in the past; and it is not everywhere so, even today.

World over, the gradations of oral literature seem to be three: among fully literate nations like those of western Europe there is a prose form enshrining folk tales and *Märchen* of considerable variety; among partly literate peoples like those of eastern Europe there may also exist traditional verse forms, narrative ballads, often remembered through many generations and begetting imitative improvisations in like genre; while among wholly illiterate (but not therefore uncivilized) races there may flourish fully organized oral literature of unrestricted range and high artistic merit, such as has existed among Norse- and Celtic- and Greek-speaking peoples. It is in this latter environment that heroic epic properly belongs.

There is thus a sort of hierarchy of oral literature, with heroic epic near the highest and children's fairy tales near the lowest place; but there is a real and great difficulty in explaining how such a hierarchy is formed. If folk tale and fairy story are the last to resist the onset of literacy, shall we say that therefore these must merely be the hardest to kill, the toughest and stoutest of oral forms, able to outlive their more susceptible kindred? or shall we maintain that they more properly resemble a band of desperate survivors making their final stand in the only stronghold still uncaptured by the enemy, so that fugitives from all ranks may be found among them—from heroic epics, songs and ballads, myths and fables and adventure stories, all reduced to the lowly guise of *Märchen*? Are modern remnants of oral literature a historical residue of all that was great and good in the illiterate past? or—to change the metaphor—are they but a feeble growth of weeds in a poor man's garden from which all the statelier flowers have long since been taken?

Even if we grant that oral literature, as a genus of human artistic expression, may be a survival out of the immeasurable past before writing was invented, it does not thereby follow that its modern content, wherever it still survives, individually shares the antiquity of its kind. The date of any given piece of oral literature is the day on which it was last recited or on which it was reduced to writing. The true and proper date of those stories which the Brothers Grimm wrote down from the lips of unlettered reciters is the beginning of the nineteenth century. Most of them were uncontaminated by written literature, whose devices they ignore. In their form and pattern they often suggest great antiquity. Yet few of the stories, as they were actually told, can be oral documents handed down unaltered from a remote past, since they so often refer their surroundings to conditions recognizably recent.

Manifestly, they have been retold to suit their narrator and audience. But how many times has this process of retelling already taken place? Some commentators, noting that stories of essentially the same content may be found dispersed over a huge area among races of very different speech, have concluded that such wide (even world-wide!) occurrence of comparable variants of a story is proof that once long ago, in a sort of primal Eden older than the Tower of Babel, there was told a primal story, an *Urmärchen,* from which all the modern counterparts are descended, like the animals of today which pious belief claims for descendants of the weirdly assorted zoölogical household afloat in Noah's ark. The theological and the folklore creed are equally naïve. But it is easier to mock the dispersion theory than to find a satisfactory substitute for it. Let us grant that the range of story patterns is limited, and that more than one mind can think the same thought and construct the same story, or even that such tales, being reflections of universal wishes, hopes, and fears, must share the sameness of all human psychology. We shall still be left with a residue of inexplicable coincidences. Probably the solution is complex—almost as complex as the folklore material itself; and we shall have to be resigned to try every case on its individual merits. We shall therefore neither maintain that all the most familiar folk tales came originally from India or the Near East or from anywhere else, nor yet hold the extreme opposite view that like begets like, that any story can spring up anywhere at any time, and that the comparative study of folk tales is merely an exploration of the behavior of the human mind. We shall admit the possibility that there can be folk tales told today which have been told in strikingly similar form not merely centuries but thousands of years ago, since there is no good objection to such tenacity of oral memory and oral transmission. We shall admit the possibility that classical Greece was not the beginning of all Western literature, since behind its literature of reed pen and papyrus, unexplored and of vast extent, may have stretched an unwritten literature which lived by tongue and memory alone.

◇ ◇ ◇

American classical learning has been fortunate in its Homeric scholars. At this university, Calhoun wrote his numerous essays on Homeric topics with unfailingly judicious reasoning and quiet charm. Among the earliest of the Sather lecturers, Scott made his incisive and militant attack on the Homeric separatists and disintegrators. His *Unity of Homer* will be read as long as there is a public for the Homeric Question. Later, Bassett made his contribution to the Sather Lectures. But perhaps the most brilliant of this distinguished company has probably remained the least heeded. Milman Parry suffered the tragic and untimely death of those whom the old Homeric gods love, but not before he had completed and published his unanswerable and unassailable proof that Iliad and Odyssey belong to the class of oral literatures—composed in the mind and not on paper, retained in the memory and not in books, recited to audiences, heard and not read. Parry's exposition must be followed with extreme attention. Even so, it will probably not prove completely intelligible to any but the professional scholar. His work—only a few pamphlets in all—will not be read, like that of Scott, by the general student of literature. But whether or not it is read at all, its truth abides almost as surely as Euclid's demonstrations abide whether or not anyone chooses to retrace their close-knit reasoning. In brief, Parry showed that Homeric verse does not work in formulas merely in order to be quaint, nor is it replete with repetitions through accident of style or contamination of text. It borrows and repeats so frequently because the very elements of speech out of which it is composed are not words but metrical phrases and complete poetical sentences. Where written literature with visual preciousness focuses the reader's attention on the individual adjective and turn of phrase, laying unceasing claim to novelty and variety, oral literature behaves like oral speech in general and recites the remarks of yesterday and yesteryear without being in the least abashed at its own uninventiveness. Only, unlike normal speech, this epic speech is metrical. For meter is mnemonic form as well as poet's privilege; and everyday language must be converted and elevated to metrical language before the oral poet can traffic in it. Such metricized speech does not thereby become an individual possession which only its creator may use: it belongs, not to all men, but to all poets and reciters. It is no one's private property any more than ordinary prose speech is anyone's special preserve. It is merely another, although somewhat specialized, idiom of communication. Its practitioners, the oral poets, learn it as the native tongue of their calling. This metrical speech—like human speech in general—is created by many, used by many, and hence belongs to many. No wonder it resembles itself, reflects itself, and reduplicates itself! Once formed, it is stubbornly preserved. But like ordinary everyday speech it slowly alters to suit shifting taste and to match new topics.

Homeric hexameter fully displays these specific qualities of oral poetic speech. Its language is not that of any Greek dialect or any group of prose speakers, because it is a metrical creation markedly altering the vernacular and preserving its own traditional expressions even when it passed from an Aeolic to an Ionic environment. Many of its grammatical inflections are peculiarly its own, being devised to suit hexametrical patterns. So formed and so inherited, its phrases and expressions felt no shame in threadbare usage, but were content to serve without pride or preciosity as the current fabric of epic speech. When the Iliad in three different passages employs identical verses to describe how a warrior

> set on his mighty head the well-made horsehair-crested
> helmet, whose plume dreadfully nodded down from above,

and the Odyssey uses these same verses to describe how Odysseus armed himself after he had exhausted his arrows against the cowering suitors, the identity proves or disproves nothing for the authorship of the poems. Whether the same or a different poet is speaking in any of the four instances, he has merely said the same thing in the same way because he has conveniently and fittingly expressed himself in the common language of his profession. The idiom of such a language does not reside in its individual words so much as in the larger cohesive metrical units. Such use of a formulaic metric language need not reduce all poetical speech to the commonplace and the reiterative, even though this is its constant danger and may be its ultimate fate—whence much of the tediousness of the later Greek epic. Within and beside the stereotyped structure there will always be opportunity for originality of expression; and if this be felicitous or striking, it will impress itself enough to be remembered and thus to survive. In many of the most memorable passages in Homer it is not the matter or wording, but the application and effect, that are new. Thus, critics have often extolled the laconic grimness with which the poet of the Odyssey hangs the unfaithful handmaidens, who

> wriggled with their feet a little while, but not for very long.

Yet the poet's genius did not lie in the invention of so devastating a description of death by the noose but rather, having already likened the women to birds caught in a fowling net, in apprehending their further resemblance to fish struggling and expiring on the line. The phrase was already made and available; he merely used it with supreme aptness.

Or again, who having once read will ever forget the proud and cruel answer of Achilles to the wretched suppliant who has clasped his knees and begged for his life?—

> Die, friend, you too die! Why do you lament so? Patroklos died, who was a better man than you. And see you not what manner of man am I

myself, how fair, how strong, I that had a hero for father and a goddess for my mother? Yet over me also hangs death, and the power of fate. A morning shall come, or an evening, or a midday, when some man shall take my life in battle with the casting of a spear or with an arrow from the bowstring.

I doubt if anyone except the scholar turning the pages of his concordance to Homer will suspect how much of that has also been used piecemeal here and there elsewhere in the poem.

Such stitching of metrical tags and recombining of phrases is not mere *cento* and patchwork: it is the legitimate and finest oral usage. By virtue of its unforgettable perfection such a passage could survive intact through many generations of reciters. And even for more routine stretches we should be surprised at the tenacity with which such poetry preserved itself from change. Those who hold that if Homer was transmitted orally for several generations we need never hope to recapture the original Homer err grievously.

When the Brothers Grimm were collecting their folk tales, they were so fortunate as to find a peasant woman with a great gift for remembering and telling the stories for which they sought so avidly. Of her they record that she recited with great sureness and confidence:

Whoever believes that tradition can easily be falsified, that carelessness will prevent preservation and hence that the duration of such tales must be brief, should have heard how exactly she kept to her story and how careful she was of its accuracy. In retelling a tale she never made a change; and if she slipped, she noticed it in time to correct it in the very moment.

This woman knew and could recite an unbelievable assortment of stories, many of them rather long.

There were no printed or written sources for such a peasant; and there were none for the makers of Iliad and Odyssey. I do not intend to argue here the highly technical and tedious question of the date of the Greek adoption of the Phoenician alphabet. But for my basic approach in these lectures I must be emphatic in declaring that the results of this controversy are by now confined within quite narrow limits of uncertainty and that the still numerous voices of the dissident no longer represent the actual state of the inquiry. It is strange how much opposition has arisen to a theorem which alone conforms with our present knowledge of the evolution of Greek civilization. No one doubts that the Mycenaean culture was literate (although no one knows how widespread was its use of a derivative Minoan form of writing). With the disintegration of the Mycenaean culture this Mycenaean script fell into disuse; no specimen of it has turned up in any Aegean environment of the first millennium B.C. In the more primitive Geometric culture which ensued, no traces of writing have been found until Geometric in turn began to give way to the Classic civilization of Greece. The new script—which in time became the common possession of all Greeks and through them reached most of the ancient Western world—is unmistakably of Phoenician derivation. And just at the time that it first appears in Greece, other cultural material such as vases and metalwork gives proof of a new and powerful contact with the civilizations of the extreme southeastern Mediterranean. During the second half of the eighth century B.C. there is a sudden introduction of Assyrian and Egyptian motifs in characteristic hybrid Phoenician form. Here, archaeologically attested, is the Phoenician phase of Greek culture. What wonder if this is the period when Phoenician alphabetic signs, too, appear in Greece?

When so good a Semitic scholar as Professor Albright of Johns Hopkins is prepared to assert that the Semitic alphabetic signs do not agree morphologically with their Greek derivatives except during the hundred years between 825 and 725 B.C., when the most painstaking sifting of the Greek epigraphical evidence has failed to turn up a single Greek written document or even a single

Greek letter-sign on clay or metal or stone that can be dated earlier than the later of these two crucial dates, when the development and spread of writing from a mere recording of proper names and brief phrases to full and normal literary use can be traced in Greece through the two centuries succeeding this critical period—then it is a forlorn prospect to continue in an obstinate conviction that the Greeks must have been a literate people from the remotest times just because the Iliad and Odyssey are literary masterpieces.

But the knowledge—gained from within—that the Homeric epics are oral compositions, and the conviction—imposed from without—that the Greeks were unable to write until the close of the eighth century before Christ, cannot be combined to yield any information on the date of composition of the Iliad and Odyssey. Because they belong to oral literature they need not therefore be older than writing. Such an inference would be faulty because oral literature can continue to flourish during and after the introduction of letters. Writing will ultimately kill it: *"ceci tuera cela!"*; but the death may be slow and lingering. In Russia, literacy and oral literature existed side by side for a thousand years.

But if we cannot thus guess the date of composition, we can at least estimate the probable time of the written recording. When letters are first introduced into a community which already practices literary composition without their aid, the new art at first serves more practical uses such as records of names, deeds, and laws. Indeed, observation has shown that laws are almost invariably the first longer texts to be constructed. In Greece the evidence is good that laws were beginning to be written out about the middle of the seventh century; hence we are entitled to infer that writing was still a comparatively novel accomplishment at that time. Further inference may be drawn from the obvious impossibility of registering such lengthy works as the Homeric epics on clay or stone or metal and the extreme historical improbability that papyrus could have been an accessible commodity among the Greeks until after the commercial exploitation of the Egyptian Delta toward the end of the seventh century B.C. This inference (which has already been drawn by such specialists as Th. Birt in his *Das antike Buchwesen*) would deny the possibility of any manuscript recording of Iliad or Odyssey until the sixth century B.C.—if only for lack of paper!

Actually, we have ancient testimony to just such a reduction of Homer to book form during precisely this period of the sixth century; but this testimony has been abused and reviled, treated as an absurd late invention, and flatly contradicted and rejected by many of the most eminent modern scholars. Yet the true situation seems rather to be that, if antiquity had neglected to record for us the Peisistratean recension of Homer, we should have to invent it for ourselves as a hypothesis essential to explain the facts. For consider what the facts are, and what the evidence demands:

The Iliad and Odyssey are earmarked as oral literature; yet we have inherited them as written books. Hence they must at some time have been reduced to writing; and this should have been done by others than the original compositors, since the makers of oral compositions are exempt from the need of such transcription. The need will arise later and only when a cherished oral transmission threatens to become confused, faulty, and unreliable. It is not beside the point to remind you of Mohammed and his great creation, the Koran. The Arab world of the seventh century of our era was literate; but it does not appear that Mohammed was very deeply versed in the craft of writing. He may have dictated substantial portions of his compositions and thus insured their existence in written form; yet after Mohammed's death there arose the fear that much of his work might be lost—which certainly implies an extensive oral transmission. The Caliph therefore commissioned a certain scribe to collect the Koran in its entirety, and according to this man's account he collated whatever he could find written on leather, ribs of palm leaves, and flat stones. But most of the great work he found within "the breasts of men" and from that perishable source rescued it, to become what it is today—"the most read book in all the world." If we apply the analogy to the Homeric epics we should expect *primâ facie* that, since the dialectic cast of the poems is unquestionably Ionic, the reduction to writing should have occurred in the homeland of their composition, the Ionian coastal and island strip of Asia Minor. But there is decisive internal evidence against such an assumption. Our standard text of Homer goes back to Athens of the fourth century before Christ, and this text in turn was demonstrably transcribed from an earlier version in the archaic Attic alphabet. This older way of writing, which established itself in Athens around the year 700 B.C., was gradually supplanted in that city during the course of the fifth century by the phonetically slightly more complete Ionic system. The process of transliteration from the older into the newer writing betrays itself in the occasional embarrassment of the scribe, who, because he was dealing with a poetic and not entirely familiar dialect, was occasionally at a loss how to interpret the ambiguities of the less complete notation. The Alexandrian schoolmen of late Greek times were perfectly aware of this vicissitude in the establishment of the Homeric texts which they expounded, and had a recognized word for this transliteration out of the older into the standard script. We may brush their word and the entire phenomenon aside in a petulant outburst, as did Wilamowitz; but it remains nonetheless and must be reckoned with and accounted for, whether we like it or not. For there it is.

How old was this older Attic text which, if the ancient account deserves credence, might claim to have been the first and original writing-down of the Homeric poems? We have noted that the earliest possible date must be the time of the opening of the Nile

Delta to Greek commercial traffic toward the close of the seventh century. But whoever carefully ponders the conditions under which oral compositions are likely to be reduced to manuscript will hesitate to champion quite so early a date. The plea that the rhapsodes who created these poems must have caused them to be written down in order to preserve them is an argument without worth, betraying total unfamiliarity with the genus of oral literature. And if the original composers or compilers felt no need of writing their verses down, neither did those who succeeded them and whose craft and livelihood it was to memorize and recite these masterworks. In a community where oral literature flourishes, there must be some special occasion or incentive to justify the otherwise pointless expenditure of energy involved in manuscript notation. The Brothers Grimm wrote down the old wives' tales in the German-speaking provinces; but the old peasant women themselves would never have done so, even had they possessed the requisite facility. Nor would their audiences have made any similar effort. Likewise in the ancient world it would not have been the rhapsodes themselves, but someone outside of their profession with a different interest and stake, who could have inaugurated so tedious a project as that of taking down on papyrus rolls nigh on thirty thousand verses to the slow tempo of carefully spelling out each word in dictation. Although Solon at the start of the sixth century might have been interested in such a task, the Ionic orientation, literary patronage, and cultural ambition of Peisistratos and his sons were so much more pronounced as to make them the only really likely sponsors of the undertaking. There is nothing here for laughter or for learned gibe, but a historic clue beyond price and beyond invention.

Modern incredulity has similarly been vented on the tradition in the pages of Pausanias that the *Works and Days* of Hesiod was incised on sheets of lead and preserved in the Vale of the Muses near the place of its composition. When Pausanias declares that he saw this unwieldy metal book, it is wiser to believe him than to doubt him. Yet we may well ask, Why on lead instead of on papyrus or parchment? Might this not be because the verses were written down in the period before the introduction of Egyptian paper, when stone and clay and metal were the normal repositories of the new "scratchings" (as the Greeks called their letter-signs)? But then this recording of Hesiod would be older than the recording of Homer. Would this be merely because the *Works and Days* is so much shorter than Iliad or Odyssey? If we look at the poem itself, another explanation will suggest itself.

The Greek epithet *rhapsode,* or "song-stitcher," admirably conveys the patchwork technique of the oral compositor, working with metrical rags and ribbons which he can sew together to make hexameters. Such a process, precisely because it dispenses with writing, could scarcely persevere without radical change if its author began to compose visually in script instead of by memory and ear. Under the eye's close scrutiny the *mot juste,* the unusual and original turn, would supplant the *mot poétique,* the merely traditional and metrically convenient epithet and phrase. The modern reader may be quick to suppose that written literature tends to length because there can be no such thing as fatigue in letters once set down, whereas oral literature should tend to brevity because every word of it must be remembered by a human brain. Yet quite the opposite is the case; for writing is slower and more arduous than speaking, and reading is a more toilsome accomplishment than reciting. So that, in defiance of what the thoughtless might imagine, early written literature (witness the earliest Greek elegiac and iambic poetry) tends to compactness and brevity, with sententious conciseness displacing colloquial loquacity, whereas mature oral epic, undismayed by what seems an impossible task to us moderns who have lost our memories through relying too much on letters, runs on like Odysseus in the Iliad, who "moved not his staff either forward or backward

... but in a great voice uttered words more thickly than winter snowflakes."

But Hesiod in the *Works and Days* does not display these traits of oral composition. He does not repeat himself; he does not use one line to build another; though he is patently familiar with Homer and occasionally echoes him, he does not work with the conventional Homeric tags, epithets, and phrases. Hesiod builds a close, almost clumsily taut line, as though he had watched each word as he wrote it down, instead of dipping generously into the garrulous ready-made speech of the rhapsodes. The abbreviated bulk, the almost niggard terseness of expression, the narrow range of plot, the style which prefers proverb and maxim to description and example, all mark out the *Works and Days* as written literature. As such, it should be the first on Greek soil. If it was written down for posterity on sheets of lead, we are entitled to conclude that it was composed before Egyptian paper was introduced into Boeotia and hence most probably before Amasis favored Greek commercial penetration of Egypt in the second quarter of the sixth century. In the other direction chronologically, we are entitled to doubt the possibility of such extensive literary exploitation of the imported Phoenician letter-signs in Boeotia much before the middle of the seventh century, even though Askra and the Vale of the Muses were near enough to be in touch with such centers of literacy as commercial Chalkis and religious Delphi. Perhaps there are internal clues in the poem by which these limits of 650–575 B.C. can be narrowed down; but if so, they are not for these lectures, which have enough to occupy us without piling Hesiod on Homer.

For us of today, the Homeric poems constitute the very beginnings of Greek literature; actually, they could not possibly have occupied that position. Rather, they must have been very near the ending (as they certainly were the finest flowering) of a long antecedent tradition of oral poetry in Greece. Were we to insist that, as its name implies, all literature must be written with letters, then Hesiod and Archilochos would begin Greek literature; but Homer would *precede* it, as a survivor from an older and different genus.

Russian ballads (*byliny*) of the so-called Kiev Cycle are still known and recited in many parts of Russia, often hundreds, even thousands, of miles from the city of Kiev. They refer specifically to matters and men of the twelfth and thirteenth centuries. They correctly remember, as leading cities of Russia, Kiev and Chernigov (then at the height of their power and in mutual rivalry). The valley of the Dnieper is still the center of their attention; and even when their modern place of survival is the far north of Russia or Siberia, their scenery is still South Russian.

Were we to assume a parallel history for the Greek oral poetry which culminated in Homer, we should be led back into Mycenaean time. We should not be surprised if Greek epic remembered that Mycenae and Thebes and Orchomenos were once the richest and most powerful cities. And if we imagined that, in addition to such historic reference to an age of exploits, the poems treasured folk tale and other persistent tribal lore, we should be entitled to look even farther, behind Mycenaean times. But such a quest would presumably not lead us whither the scrutiny of Mycenaean art and material culture usually leads—to Crete and ancient Anatolia. For the Greeks' own tradition about their poetry was precise and unambiguous. There is no Minoan or Asianic blood in the veins of the Grecian Muses. Whether of Helikon and Parnassos or of Pieria below Olympos, whether Hellenic or "Thracian," they dwelt remote from the Cretan-Mycenaean world and in touch with the *European* elements of Greek speech and culture.

Thus, behind Mycenaean Greece—provided we are dealing in language, poetic craft, folk tale, tribal tradition, rather than in art, material culture, or religious cults—lies Europe. Hence in these lectures I shall employ the unfashionable hypothesis that the ultimate sources should be the same for Greek epic as for the rest of western Europe. On this assumption, the generous discrepancy of time between Homer and Beowulf need not be as significant as the even more remote identity of their oral tradition; and the difference in medium between the stately Ionic epic and the humble *Kinder- und Hausmärchen* may not be so crucial as the community of cultural heritage in Hellene and Teuton.

Is it really so fantastic to maintain that the Hänsel and Gretel story may be as old as the Odyssey, or even older? or that so supreme a literary artist as Homer could have drawn on the same material as a modern peasant storyteller? Let us only suppose that each somehow did have access to the same widely known and widely told traditional store and that each had converted the same folk tale to the setting and social level of his own environment; in short, to the only world of his immediate knowledge. Would it not follow that in the tale for children the heroes might be children, and in the peasant's world the setting would be a peasant setting of forest and penurious woodchoppers, while Homer would necessarily have worked otherwise, till nothing of the mid-European tale but had suffered a sea change—a Mediterranean and Hellenic sea change—into the something rich and strange which was the tale of Troy's heroes and the sunlit world of the Greek heroic epic?

We may readily convince ourselves that such an episode as that of Circe cannot have been invented by the author of the Odyssey. From the viewpoint of fairy lore, several incidents in the story have been mistold. And some of the setting suggests the deep forest-land of Europe rather than the rocks and mountains of a Mediterranean island. "Hearken now unto my words," says Odysseus to his much-suffering companions; "we know not where is darkness nor where is dawn, nor where the sun, who lightens mortals, goes under earth nor yet where he moves aloft."

No Grecian mariner on the midland sea could thus have lost his celestial bearings. These are the words of a landsman wandering vaguely in great dark woods. And in the poem there is indeed "thicket and wood" to cover Circe's seagirt isle. In the very heart of the forest, in a clearing among the glades, was built the witch's house. In fairy tale there are two ways to find this dread and hidden spot, which is of course utterly remote from the paths of men: it may be sighted by climbing an unusually tall tree; or some wonderful animal, pursued witlessly, will lead the wanderer to it. In the Odyssey both devices are employed. Odysseus, mounting a craggy lookout, thence catches glimpses of smoke arising; and as he descends again toward his comrades on the shore, some god who took pity on his lone wandering sends a marvelously great antlered stag across his path. But the hero knows nothing better to do than to kill the animal and carry it, though it was really too heavy for carrying, to make a day's feasting for his ship's company. Thereafter half his crew sets out for the smoke beacon in the forest and duly reaches the clearing with its lonely house. At their call the beautiful witch, whom they have heard singing within, promptly appears at the door and bids them in. They drink of what she offers, and are helpless. Perhaps Homer deemed it obvious that swine are reared to be devoured; yet I find it strange that there is neither direct mention nor hint of Circe's sinister intentions in transforming her visitors and penning them within her sties. Odysseus' lieutenant, Eurylochos, even imagines that the poor fawning wolves and lions are there "to guard the great house under compulsion," as though the witch with her terrible magic were in need of protection! It is Eurylochos who by his suspicion avoids the fate of the rest of his company and returns alone to the ship with news of presumed calamity. Odysseus picks up sword and bow and goes to the rescue. Close by the clearing in the forest a young man meets him—not a little, bearded, old man or a dwarf, as fairy lore would have told it, but the god Hermes, the dead man's guide, in mortal shape. He hands him the magic plant *moly* of dark root and milk-white flower, which mortals scarce may dig; but Odysseus seems totally to forget this charm when he meets the witch, and Homer (who displays the classic Greek's characteristic failure to comprehend faërie) never bothers to mention it again. May we not guess that the magic flower once had a more prominent and more effective place in the story, and that the story itself was older than Odysseus' telling of it? And if no further word enlightens us on the ultimate fate of the "mountain-bred wolves and lions" roaming outside Circe's house, though they too must have been enchanted human beings, may we not draw the same conclusion that a proper fairy tale preceded and was the source for this episode in the Odyssey and that, in exact reverse of Circe's witchcraft, it had lost its magic shape and assumed human form at the touch of Homer's wand?

Again, it belongs to a certain folk-tale pattern that the villain, when overcome by the hero, should admit to having known beforehand the identity of his victorious adversary, but should have failed to recognize him in time to elude him. Just so, after Polyphemos has been blinded, he recalls how a soothsayer among the Cyclopes had told him long before

> how all these things should come to pass and how I should be deprived of sight at the hands of Odysseus; but always I anticipated some hero great and fair would come hither, instead of a little good-for-nothing weakling.

And in similar vein, hardly is Circe forced to yield to her unsorcerable assailant, when she cries,

> Who and whence art thou of mortals? Surely, thou art the resourceful Odysseus whom the golden-wanded Argos-slayer ever told me would come!

Whence came this gratuitous touch of folklore unless out of the great universal tradition of folk tale, to which Homer must have had access?

Or what value shall we attach to the observation that Odysseus in the Cyclops' cave, having decided not to try to kill the ogre with his sword, by good chance discovers a fitter weapon in the huge olivewood cudgel "like in size to the mast of a dark twenty-oared vessel," which Polyphemos had cut "to carry when it should have seasoned"? How well that is all motivated! Odysseus refrains from putting the giant to the sword, since otherwise he and his comrades would have been trapped in the cave, unable to roll the mighty stone away from its opening (yet he could equally well have blinded him with the swordpoint!); and the great club is available, and not out and away on the uplands in its master's hands when he goes forth for the day, because it is still too green for use. Is it possible that a plausible Greek has here been rationalizing fairy lore much older than his own enlightened Ionian brain? For it belongs to a certain folk-tale motif that the monster cannot be slain by ordinary human means, but only by some special weapon of his own, which by good luck or superior knowledge may be discovered somewhere in his fearful haunt. So, to quote one instance among many, in the Early English poem of Beowulf, when its hero has plunged beneath the mere into the underwater home of Grendel, his sword which had never before failed him proves useless against the she-troll whom he finds there. At the last moment, with the horrible hag kneeling on him and her dagger trying to pierce his steel corselet, he struggles to his feet and catches sight of a giant sword amid the pile of Grendel's war gear, "the fairest of weapons, hanging on wall." This he seizes and swings, though it was so heavy no hand but his could hold it, and, striking at the troll's throat in the fury of despair, kills her on the instant.

But it is not only the Odyssey with its fanciful tales which thus betrays a trafficking with fairyland and the magic *Märchen*-world. In the Iliad, Achilles' choice between two fates which bear him deathward, whether to gain imperishable fame at expense of a short life or long life at expense of slight renown, belongs to folk tale. So does his comprehension of his horse's speech, foretelling him doom as he takes him into battle. To fairy lore belong also his marvelous weapons, the ashen spear which "none other of the Greeks could wield," the divine armor forged by Hephaistos, and the cloud of fire that burns around his head. When the gods wrap their favorites in mist and make them invisible upon the battlefield or snatch them suddenly away to city or camp, this too is fairy-tale mechanism and smacks of witchcraft quite as strong as though the heroes had clapped on their heads the famous *Tarnkappe,* the cap of invisibility—which, incidentally, Greek myth knows well and calls correctly by name.

How can such palpable make-believe, such reminiscences from the impossible world of fairy story, find place in an epic account of a great enterprise which purports to be history and attaches to the actual Greek world with its well-known towns, districts, and islands? It can do so for the very simple reason that such is the normal and natural way of oral epic. Saga, which purports to be true fact and happening held fast in popular memory; fiction, which is the persuasive decking out of circumstance with trappings borrowed from contemporary actuality; and folk tale, which is utterly unreal but by no means utterly irrational—all these can be sewn together in the rhapsode's glittering fabric.

If we would really understand Homer, we first must study these.

CHAPTER II

SAGA AND FICTION

THE ANCIENT classical world displayed, almost without exception, an extreme credulity toward the Homeric narrative. One might suppose that the Peloponnesian War with all the firsthand documentation of Thucydides was no whit more real a historical event to the Greeks and Romans than the legendary expedition of the Argives and Achaeans to recapture Helen from the Trojans. Because of its accepted authority, a single verse from the Iliad might be crucial in a boundary dispute between adjacent towns; and in almost any discussion the verdict of Homer could claim to rank as a final court of appeal. Clearly, the Greeks believed that Homer's account was a record of actual events in which the heroic past of their own tribes and towns was narrated. For them, the Trojan War was a landmark as sure as the First Olympiad and as indisputable as the Persian invasion; Agamemnon of Mycenae enjoyed as excellent a historical status as Kypselos of Corinth, Nestor as Solon the Wise, Ajax as Milo the Strong.

But the modern world, noting the abundance and variety of contemporary written record for Greek political history during the last five centuries before Christ as against the singleness of epic testimony and the temporal remoteness of its pretended narrative, inclined to an ever-growing skepticism which culminated during the nineteenth century in complete disbelief in Troy and all things Trojan or Achaean. Helen the Fair, hatched from a swan's egg, was a myth quite as palpably as her twin brothers the Dioskouroi, who shine as stars in the heaven and come to the aid of storm-wracked mariners. In her name (it was held) there was hidden the same root of "brightness" which appeared in the Greek word for moon—the moon which has the morning and evening stars for attendants, yet is somehow stolen away and disappears from between them. If Helen was only a moon myth, the warriors who rescued her were only a poet's evocation, literary heroes performing chivalresque deeds, human counterparts to their imaginary gods. After all, Homer himself did not pretend to have seen these wonderful events nor to have lived in their time, but admitted frankly that men had degenerated greatly from those heroic days of which he sang, and appealed to a poetic Muse to tell him what to say about such far-off things, in clear confession that their distance and their greatness were the mirage of poetic fancy:

> Tell me now, ye Muses with homes on Olympos,
> Since ye are divine, ever-present, and all things knowing,
> While *we* hear but rumor, ourselves knowing nothing!

Then came Schliemann with his incredible excavations of Troy and Tiryns and Mycenae.

On the edge of the Trojan plain, some three miles from the ancient Hellespont which modern maps call the Dardanelles, there lay meager traces of the Roman city of Ilium. Here the self-schooled enthusiast, Heinrich Schliemann, gathered Turkish workmen and dug deep into a conspicuous truncated cone of a hill, irreparably destroying much that he uncovered, but at least making it plain that under Roman and Greek classical levels there still lay buried the house foundations and protecting girdle walls of a prehistoric citadel. That was in the 1870's. By the end of the decade, "the treasure-digger of the first campaign had turned into the conscientious excavator with a sense of his responsibilities for professional exploration and exact recording of layers and levels." Seven ruined cities lay one above the other in the mound of Ilion-Hissarlik; and one among these must be an actual remnant of Homer's Troy. So thought Schliemann and so, after a brief startled and rebellious gasp, thought almost all educated opinion in late nineteenth-century Europe.

At Mycenae the discoveries were even more sensational. Within the Lions' Gate, where tourist and sightseer had trodden for generations, the chieftains of the ancient stronghold still lay underground in their graves, with golden masks and ornaments, inlaid daggers, cups and jewelry in such profusion as might almost have befitted a pharaoh of Egypt. Schliemann had but to lift the soil away to bring this treasure trove back to the sunlight to dazzle the eyes of antiquary and layman alike. As over his Trojan discoveries, so over these of Mycenae incredulity strove with enthusiasm, and debate for a time ran high. But in the end it was admitted that the truth must be even as Schliemann maintained: these golden burials belonged to a civilization older than the Greeks and (so far as such temporal distances lent themselves to exactness) coeval with those very Achaean dynasties which Homer had claimed for his story.

So it was true, after all! Earlier than the classic era there had been another flowering of civilization in Greece; and at that time Mycenae had indeed been "rich in gold," as the Homeric epithet asserted; at Troy there had been a fortress town with "palaces," upon a steep above the river plain. And although little or nothing turned up to reward the digger at Odysseus' isle of Ithaca, one by one the other centers of epic legend—Tiryns, Thebes, Argos, Amyclae (though hardly Sparta),—together with the "beehive" tombs in Attica, Lacedaemon, and Triphylia, contributed their share of evidence for an Age of Heroes ruling Greece a thousand years before the final culmination of the classic epoch. Since it was impossible that Homer's identification of precisely these places as centers of "Achaean" civilization should have been sheer coincidence or necromancy, their traditions must have reached him directly from mouth to mouth through the intervening generations. Hence, the great expedition of these cities against Troy, the taking of that town after long siege, the scattering and difficult homecoming of the conquerors—all these were likewise an inheritance of actuality, a telling of true events, however long ago.

The Iliad was saga directly transmitted; the epic poems were the Greeks' own knowledge about their past, just as they themselves had always maintained.

The Catalogue of Ships—that pitilessly prosaic enumeration of Greek towns and leaders of the expeditionary force which, with its slighter Trojan counterpart, takes up nearly half of the second book of the Iliad—now became a venerable document deriving from the second millennium B.C. and thereby our oldest literary record of the Grecian world. Homer himself, though scarcely (in view of his own admissions) a Mycenaean man, now seemed to have been capable of living much earlier than had been previously supposed. A court minstrel in the baronial halls of the Early Ionian nobility—and here the new enthusiasm ran rather far ahead of the excavator's evidence and helped itself to feudal and romantic notions—might have inherited and kept alive the glamour and gossip of the immediately preceding Mycenaean courts.

It should be said at once that such excessive historization of the Greek epic was rather narrowly confined to the picturesque English school of Homeric scholarship, while German reactions took a different turn. The now tangible actuality of the Mycenaean Age, together with the archaeological demonstration of the fullness of its collapse and the long dearth and alien cultural temper of the succeeding centuries, convinced the German mind of the chronological complexity of the Homeric problem. If Homer lived close to his recorded events, then he did not live close to classical times, and our current Greek version of his compositions must have undergone all manner of change, corruption, and reformation; whereas if Homer lived nearer to the times of his classical Greek audience or was himself a classical Greek, then again the poetic tradition to which he gave final form must already have passed through centuries of vicissitude.

In any event, of this much we could all be sure: Schliemann

and Doerpfeld and his successors who created Helladic archaeology had confirmed the authenticity of the Homeric tradition, since no one could any longer doubt that, if the Homeric narrative refers to an actual world and to actual events, that world must be the one which the excavators had discovered and those events must belong to the period of the latter half of the second millennium before Christ.

It is strange how slow modern scholarship has been to admit that although such a formulation is unobjectionably correct there is a deadly sting in one of its essential words. The Homeric narrative *refers* to the Mycenaean culture, certainly; but so does Aeschylos' *Oresteia*! and in any literature there may be an abysmal division between the cultural reference and the cultural context. Thus, Shakespeare's *Julius Caesar* refers to Rome of the Late Republic; but it must use the language of Elizabethan England with all its associations, and it may not merely reflect unconsciously, it may even introduce deliberately, contemporary English ideas and cultural material. Similarly, the cultural *reference* of both Iliad and Odyssey is Achaean, and Achaean may perfectly well be Mycenaean, Late Helladic; yet their cultural *context* need not have been equally ancient. We have no logical warrant for assuming without further proof that Homer must have known more than Aeschylos about Mycenae's royal household, just because Ionic epic preceded Attic drama.

Since we of today assert that we have acquired a sizable amount of direct material information about the Mycenaean civilization (which we call Late Helladic), it has become entirely feasible for us to check on Homeric cultural and descriptive material detail and prove that the epic poets knew next to nothing about the civilization amid which they set their scenes.

Thus, the Iliad ascribes to Troy temples which house cult images of the gods, and presumably imagines the Achaean Greeks to have possessed similar structures: we are convinced that there were no temples, and think it most probable that there were no life-size cult statues, in Helladic times.

The Iliad seems to hold that the Achaeans could neither read nor write, being without means of communicating through written messages. Its warriors make only marks as symbols on the lots which they cast, and in nine long years no one ever thinks of writing a letter back home to Argos. Only in the Bellerophon story is there allusion to a written message; and here the reference is so veiled and cryptic as to suggest that, while it was necessary to the story, it was felt by the poet to be anachronistic and out of tradition. We on the other hand are convinced that the Mycenaean culture was literate, since we have dug up tablets and other objects of clay inscribed with its writing.

Homer believed that the Achaean warriors normally wore suits of bronze armor, consisting of crested helmet, breastplate, and leggings, much like the accouterment of the classical hoplite: we are convinced that they did not.

Homer is silent about inlaid designs in gold and silver for sword and dagger blades; yet in describing the new and wonderful armor of Achilles he had such a perfect opportunity for introducing these Mycenaean marvels that his failure to avail himself thereof must persuade us that he knew nothing of them.

Under Minoan influence, Mycenaean female costume was elaborate, bizarre, sensational, while the male costume was at least distinctive: the experts qualified in such matters find that Homer knows nothing of such unclassical peculiarities, but deals exclusively in early classical Greek apparel. His brooches and hairdress are equally un-Mycenaean. Nor does he ever mention finger rings and engraved seal stones, by which the Mycenaeans set unusual store.

We know that the Helladic palaces were brilliant with human figures and decorative scenes painted in bright colors on their walls: Homer has never even heard of wall painting, else he would not so utterly have omitted it from his more ambitious architectural descriptions. Neither does he betray any familiarity with the beautiful craft of glazing terra cotta.

His ideas of burial are at variance with the Mycenaean; and he never refers to the great vaulted stone tombs, which are the prime achievement of the Mycenaean builders.

As for the palaces in which his chieftains dwell, the more he goes into detail (as for Odysseus' house in Ithaca) the more apparent it becomes that their imagined plan depends, like that of the classical house, on courtyard, colonnaded vestibule, and inner room, with the women's quarters in an upper story, and shows none of the features of the intricately laid-out structures which the Helladic excavators have uncovered, with their dog-leg corridors around complex room blocks, their light wells and clerestories and broad winding staircases and heavily defended casemates. Only the bathroom, so characteristically Minoan-Mycenaean, might seem to ring true; but alas, the Homeric text really says nothing of bathrooms, but only takes its heroes to the "well-polished tub"!

So it goes through all the archaeological gamut. Professor Nilsson in his admirable *Homer and Mycenae* has faithfully sought for Mycenaean *realia* in the Homeric epic; yet the unclassical and indubitably Helladic final residue after his sifting of Homer consists, even for him, of only four items: a movable metal collar to hold the bronze spearhead firm on its wooden shaft; a remarkable gold cup which Nestor has carried with him to the war; a helmet made of wild boars' teeth sewn over a framework of leather thongs, which Odysseus once wears in the Iliad; and lastly, a frieze of a mysterious substance called *cyanos,* which adorns the palace of the Phaiakian king in the Odyssey. Save for the helmet of boars' teeth—which even for Homer is an heirloom and an antique curiosity—all of these identifications can be effectively challenged.

1) Greek spears down to Hellenistic times show a ring or collar below the spear point, cast in one piece with it and hence admittedly atrophied from a structural to a decorative element. This collar could easily have been gilded, in which case it is debatable whether it would not have served as sufficient prototype and inspiration for Hector's weapon in the Iliad. In any case, it is not the existence of this collar but its *detachability* which forms the issue, and this makes of it a very minor candidate for a Mycenaean survival in Homer.

2) The description of Nestor's cup should be read without prior conviction that it must resemble the cup from the shaft grave at Mycenae. It was a huge affair, heavier than an ordinary man could lift from the table. It had four handles and two supports, props, or bases (whatever that may mean). On or beside each handle were two doves. The shaft-grave cup has a little gold hawk attached to each of its two handles, but seems to me to present no common terms other than this use of birds as a decorative motif. The gold strips which run from either handle to the base are very extraordinary and distinctive, but they cannot be the πυθμένες of Nestor's cup, which had only two, despite its *four* handles. I am inclined to think that the archaeologists may be at fault in taking this cup too literally. There may be only literary exaggeration: in order to ascribe impressive properties to this *Ur*-tankard, where the ordinary cup has two handles it has been given four, and where the ordinary cup has only a single base it has two.

3) *Cyanos* (as Nilsson remarks) signifies lapis lazuli in later Greek; and the Mycenaean palace at Tiryns had blue glass paste incrustations decorating an ornamental member which (to judge from its recurrence on a signet ring from Tiryns) should have been a wall base or *dado*. But the comparison with the frieze of the Odyssey is specious, because (*a*) in *Homeric* Greek *cyanos* seems to be black, not faïence blue or cerulean, being applied adjectivally to the eyebrows of Zeus and the hair of Hector, neither

of which could have been of lapis lazuli hue; and (*b*) the *cyanos* frieze (θριγκός) on the palace of Alkinoos seems to have been an exterior coping or eaves above the brazen walls, so that its nature (though uncertain) has nothing demonstrably in common with the Mycenaean interior ornamental member.

We are left with a single helmet constructed of boars' teeth; and if that is really all that Homer knows about the material actualities of the great Late Helladic culture, it is tantamount to nothing at all.* How, then, does he give to every reader an impression of being so well informed and so perfectly at home in Achaean surroundings? He does so because of his craft and professional adroitness, because Saga seems to live only as Fiction recreates it. And he succeeds also because we, his readers, are in general even more ignorant than he was about the actualities of the Mycenaean epoch.

When Homer tells us that high in a clearing on the island of Ithaca the swineherd Eumaios had dragged stones for a wall to enclose a courtyard and had "coped it with a fence of white thorn, and split an oak to its dark core into stakes which he might set close on either hand," we realize that the seeming actuality of the structure comes from the poet's knowledge of how such compounds are built and not by any chance from some century-old word-of-mouth description of anything that ever stood on Ithaca in Mycenaean times. It is this direct borrowing from the poet's own experience and from his own surrounding material world that I am terming Fiction. It is this which makes his re-creation of the heroic past seem so immediately present and so vivid. Indeed, since it is fiction which imparts verisimilitude to his scenes, we may say without fear of paradox that the more real they seem

* True survivals from pre-Hellenic times seem to me to be such matters as the tendency of the gods to take on the guise of birds, the confused tradition of the use of chariots in battles, and the uncertain conviction that dead bodies can be preserved from decay by some sort of embalming. These are all likely to be poets' inheritance and prove no direct familiarity with Mycenaean conditions.

the more fictional they are. We may even make of this a theorem to assert that the more an oral poet seems to know about a distant event the less he really knows about it and the more certainly he is inventing.

The Greek historian Ephoros understood and formulated this principle very satisfactorily when he declared,

> In the case of contemporary happenings we think those witnesses the most reliable who give the greatest detail, whereas in the case of events long ago we hold that those who thus go into detail are the least to be believed, since we consider it highly improbable that the actions and words of men should be remembered at such length.

Herein lies a most vital distinction between saga and fiction. The one derives from the past, while the other is mainly dependent on the present. The one is received from afar by relay from generation to generation and grows progressively vaguer, more confused, less accurate; the other is created directly out of immediate experience and visible environment, and if it is altered, may thereby become yet the more up-to-date and real.

To an Ionian poet living in the ninth or eighth or seventh century B.C. the appearance and behavior of the Mycenaean culture was hearsay, oral tradition three or four or five hundred years old—what I am calling Saga. We may well be skeptical of the extent or accuracy of anything such Saga had to tell, particularly when we have once observed the use that oral literature generally makes of its saga material. Certain great events, certain picturesque or important persons, the leading drift and trend of the times, with here and there some poignant detail still adhering—these might properly have been the sum and substance of its information. When a poet used such tradition for plot or setting of his verses, he would have to make its shadowy remoteness present and vivid by filling in its details and *décor* and illuminating its dark unsubstantiality with the sharply clear world of his own experience and time.

Where the basic cultural environment has changed between the saga world of reference and the poet's own world of experience, the discrepancy will usually be obvious. Homer did not know what battle-chariots were for, since his own community did not use them. Hence he depicts them preposterously as mere means of local transportation to and from the actual fight. His heroes are gravely driven from their cabins on the shore to the place of contest, seldom more than a mile or two away, and there they dismount and do battle while the charioteer waits close at hand to take them home again or move them to some other contest. For this convenience they brought their horses in their crowded ships all the way from Greece! How different this is from the homely detail of the returning warriors who stand where the sea breeze from the Hellespont can dry the sweat out of their shirts, and how much more persuasive is such fiction out of immediate experience! Again, Homer makes too much mention of iron, which was an extreme rarity in the Helladic culture. Oral tradition, in the form of stock poetic phrases and verses, had apparently tied the notion of bronze inextricably to sword blades, which the classical culture naturally wrought out of iron; hence the Homeric heroes fight with swords of bronze. But seemingly there was no such tradition for chains and fetters, so that it may never have occurred to the poet that these could have been made out of any other material than iron (in which he was perhaps correct!); whereas his inherited poetic formulas, conflicting with his own everyday experience, left him hesitant from which of the two materials such things as axes, hatchets, pruning hooks, and knives should be made. The Higher Criticism has made sad havoc out of this purely literary dilemma.

Other matters, being more fundamental, were less liable to change with the shift from Mycenaean to Early Classical and hence betray no discrepancy between the poet and his theme. As Thucydides ruefully noted, human nature persists the same through the ages. But the source of an even more powerful illusion of reality is the durability of the physical geographic setting. Since Homer knew so intimately the Grecian land, the Grecian sea, the mountains and the skies, the islands and the shores, he could project his heroic characters into a world so real that they too must seem realities.

Perhaps one might expect a maker of epic verses to sketch-in his local scenery out of his fancy, much as Homer built the swineherd's courtyard on Ithaca or Achilles' cabin on the Hellespont, with details chosen for their picturesqueness or plausibility rather than for their local accuracy. But in matters of topography a Greek poet had to reckon with a Greek audience possessing an equally exact knowledge. If he sang of Lesbos, it could not be some heroically unreachable sagaland, nor yet (as for Byron) some romantic isle where burning Sappho lived and sung, but only and precisely the bit of seagirt land which still lay in the fold of the Aeolic coast. If Tenedos he said, then Tenedos it must be. If ever one sailed across from Lesbos to mainland Greece, one would make landfall of the high southernmost mountains of the island of Euboea, and one could lay the course either direct through open sea by holding north of the little island of Psyra off Chios or one could first go south through the Chian strait and then have a narrower stretch of open water to traverse. This would still be the choice if one were sailing the Aegean today: it was true for Homer's time, and he makes it true for his epic heroes. When Nestor recounts the homecoming of the Greek chieftains after the sack of Troy, he expressly mentions how they debated this alternative. In short, this heroic saga plays in the Greeks' own world, and the poet is fully aware that, in order to make his narrative vivid and convincing, he must himself be familiar with every landmark which he cites.

What, then, of Troy and the rest of the Iliad's familiar local scenery?

Let it be said at once that no informed reader has ever doubted the actuality of its geographic setting. The larger landmarks are those of a well-known sector of the northeastern Aegean. Its islands are expressly named—Samothrace (which is called Thracian Samos), Lemnos and Imbros, tiny Tenedos and sizable Lesbos. The Greek ships are drawn on the shore of the Hellespont. Among near-by mainland towns are mentioned Abydos at the narrows, Arisbe, Chryse on the sea, Zelea on the Propontis. We are dealing with an actual region accessible to any Greek. There cannot be any question of the whereabouts of the Trojan plain which forms the field of battle, since its situation and much of its local conformation appear with unambiguous immediacy from the language of the poem itself. From the text alone we may gather a fairly extensive picture of Trojan topography.

And if with this picture still fresh before us we can find occasion to visit the extreme northwest corner of the modern land of Turkey in Asia Minor, just where the strait of the Dardanelles debouches into the Aegean Sea, we shall find that picture actualized in all its natural detail. We shall find precisely such a shoreland, such a deep plain, dusty and sparsely green, with such a river running through it, as the Iliad requires. Here, then, is the long, wide strand beside the Hellespont for the Greek ships to be drawn and the Greek encampment to be set. Here is the reed-fringed river in the sun-baked plain, with expanse enough for marching footfolk and the chariots of their leaders. Homer's clear and concise setting for the Iliad still exists today. Somewhere here on a sloping rise of land at the edge of this open alluvial plain lay the object of all the expedition, the heavily walled, high-summited citadel of Troy.

It would seem natural, almost necessary, to assume that so much topographical detail could not be based on mere hearsay: in short, that Homer himself had been to Troy. Certainly, his account of events and incidents has none of the sketchy indefiniteness which distinguishes the landscapes of pure saga, wherein only that is known which has somehow failed to slip through the meshes of the great sieve of word-to-mouth repetition. Yet how shall we know for certain that all the descriptions and details, the landmarks and the moves and countermoves among them, were recounted by one who knew precisely the distances and the contours and the directions, or for that matter felt any compulsion to fit his narrative to a real terrain? The Iliad itself will give us an opportunity to answer both these questions.

In the thirteenth book it is recounted how Poseidon seated himself on the highest peak of wooded Samothrace "whence all Ida was visible and the city of Priam and the ships of the Achaeans." From his classical atlas the homekeeping scholar will discover that there is another island, Imbros, which interposes its 2,000-foot ridges between Samothrace and Troy to shut off the view, and will conclude that Homer was factually in error, having lightly assumed a possibility which neither he nor his hearers would ever put to the test. But the visitor to Troy is startled and delighted to discover on a clear day over a notched shoulder of intervening Imbros the sharp 5,000-foot peak of Samothrace. And he will turn again to his Iliad, knowing with what precise accuracy was composed the verse which put Poseidon, not vaguely somewhere on Samothrace, but exactly "on the topmost peak of wooded Samos" to look at Troy. Since no ancient climbed such tedious summits for the view, but left them to his gods, Homer must have known that Poseidon on the peak of Samothrace could have seen Troy because he himself had observed and remembered that from Troy one could see the peak of Samothrace.

Our second query, whether the author of the Iliad really felt any need of scrupulous adherence to topographic accuracy, is answered by a passage equally enlightening. During the term of Achilles' angry withdrawal from combat, the tide of battle has set against the Achaeans, who are driven back to their ships on the beach. Thus thrown on the defensive, they strengthen their position by building a great moated wall squarely across the plain and therewith convert their shore encampment into an effective stronghold. The task, which is performed under cover of a truce to gather and burn the dead, is on such a scale as to leave a lasting scar on the Scamander plain. But the poet, whose tactical invention created the whole incident, was well aware that actually there was not the slightest sign of such a mounded dike near the Hellespont. The extraordinary thing is that this so troubled his literary conscience that he inserted into his poem a careful explanation of the subsequent disappearance of this landmark. The Greeks (said he), in digging and heaping it, failed to assure the protection of the gods by sacrifice; wherefore the gods were wroth against the structure, and after the Greeks had sacked Troy (an event, it should be noted, that the normal narrative of the Iliad never reaches) and gone home in their ships to Greece, "then counsel took Poseidon and Apollo to raze the wall by bringing the might of rivers in, as many as from Ida's mount flow seaward." Homer lists all eight of these streams and insists against all orographic possibility that they were united by Apollo into a single mighty flood which raged against the moated wall for nine days and nights, "while Zeus rained incessant, to float that wall upon the sea," and Poseidon the earth-quaker, with trident in hand, brought up the might of his waves and rolled away the beams and boulders until the whole lay level with the swift Hellespont and the sand of the seabeaches hid every trace of the heroic enterprise.

Is not this conclusive evidence that Homer treated the topography of his narrative with an almost painful exactitude? Why else should he worry lest any of his hearers might object if, after so many intervening centuries, there was nothing to be seen of the great moat and wall across the plain? Judging by such punctiliousness, we must conclude that any ancient visitor would have found the other landmarks accurately disposed and described. The more intimately he was familiar with the plain of the Scamander, the more comprehensively could he enjoy every situation and every incident of the narrative. Homer's poem is the product of a mind completely informed of the exterior physical setting which he has accepted for his story and anxious to treat it with completely literal accuracy.

Is it conceivable that a Greek poet would approach a legendary theme, in which he must have been free to invent many of his characters and incidents, with such slavish submission to topographic realism? Let us look around elsewhere than in Greece and see how saga is treated and how the past is revivified by appeal to present knowledge.

◇ ◇ ◇

On any large-scale map of Iceland may be found at the west of the northern coast the deeply indented bays, fed by short streams from steep-pitched dells, where are laid the scenes of the Icelandic prose saga of Grettir the Outlaw. In Skagafirth is still to be seen the tiny island of Drang with its sheer cliffs atop of which Grettir bided his outlawry. Farther west at the head of Midfirth are the steadings where he was born; and eastward therefrom over Willowdale (Vididalr) beyond the cluster of little meres lies Shadowvale (Forsaeludalr) running up from Waterdale (Vatnsdalr)—just as the saga tells. So, with the Grettir story in one's knapsack, one can follow the splendid tale about, and still today find all the places where its heavy-handed hero spent his unhappy and unruly life. Just as its topography is genuine, so the majority of its characters, whether the scene is laid in Iceland or in Norway, appear to be actual historical persons. And all the main externals of Grettir's lifetime as the saga records them can be fitted correctly into the early decades of the eleventh century of our era, when Olaf the Saint was king of Norway and Skapti Thorodson of Hjalli was lawman in Iceland. The saga was probably written down some two and a half centuries after the events which it narrates. Being based on oral tradition, it deals with actual men and makes their doings vivid by a firsthand knowledge of the country and direct appeal to a culture still familiar to the saga-teller. But though many of the events may be real, the chief characters have surely grown in dramatic stature and taken on heroic proportions for good and evil. And much that never belonged to them has been drawn to them, somewhat as iron filings arrange themselves to concordant patterns under a powerful magnet. Thus, Shadowvale and Waterdale are real enough; but what Grettir did there at Thorhallstead belongs to folk tale, not to saga, since his wrestling with Glam's ghost in the ruined hall matches point for point Beowulf's struggle with the monster Grendel in the mead hall of Heorot in Denmark; and later in the story, when Grettir wrestles with the huge troll-wife and strikes off her arm, then dives under the waterfall to kill the giant in the cave, there are telltale features that leave no doubt that this is again the same story along with that of Grendel's dam and the dismal pool of the Old English epic. Folk tale and historic saga and literary fiction all blend harmoniously into the reality of the bleak Icelandic world wherein the sagateller lived.

There is a remarkable opportunity for checking epic elaboration against historical reality by exploring the chronicles of Charlemagne and setting them against the epic assertions of the Song of Roland. In the medieval French poem, Charlemagne after seven years of battle against the Saracens has conquered all of Spain except the city of Saragossa. Actually and historically, the situation was quite other. Having overrun only a fringe of the country, Charlemagne in the year 778 was wondering what to do against Saragossa when word was brought to him that at home in the Rhineland the Saxons had risen in revolt. He was consequently forced to abandon his Spanish campaign and return north to deal with the situation there. On the return march, his rear guard was ambuscaded by certain "Wascons" (who might be Basques or Gascons) and in the encounter there were slain (according to the contemporary *Vita Karoli Magni* of Einhard) "Eggihard, that was in charge of the king's table; Anselm, a chamberlain of the king's household; and Hruodland, margrave of the Brittany Marches." The "Wascons," being familiar with the country and aided by nightfall, scattered and escaped. That is probably all that really happened. Roland, as Hruodland, prefect of the Breton March, is thus a strictly historical character, and his death in a rear-guard incident of Charlemagne's retirement in midsummer of A.D. 778 is equally authentic. Out of this comparatively unimportant event the epic legend expanded the form and substance of a magnificent heroic exploit. Who does not remember the tale? the treacherous Ganelon conspiring with the Saracens and maneuvering his detested stepson Roland into command of the rear guard, and then—the pass of Roncevaux, the huge Saracenic force cutting off the detachment of twenty thousand men under Roland, Oliver, and his twelve peers, Roland's refusal to sound his horn for aid until only sixty of his side are left, and finally, himself fatally wounded, the only one still alive of all his company, using his last breath to blow his horn and, as he dies, hearing the answering trumpet-calls of Charlemagne returning in overwhelming force to avenge him on the Saracen! This is epic imagination at its finest. But who that tried to work backward from the poetical account to the actual historical event (unless he looked into Einhard's chronicle) could ever guess how much the scale must shrink and how little can remain of the mighty Frankish battle against the pagan horde?

Precisely because the warfare in the poem is fictitious it offers an opportunity for investigating strategy and tactics as the poetic military imagination conceives them. By strict definition there is none: a series of single combats glorifying the personal prowess of Roland and Oliver and the peers is made to carry all the action of battle. But is not this also the state of affairs in the Iliad, where the common footfolk are merely a vague surging background against which the illustrious heroes meet in single fray as each of the champions (or may we call them paladins?) takes his turn under the epic spotlight? Could we have a more striking indication that the incidents of battle on the Scamander plain originated in the same epic workshop of a poet's brain as the battle at the Pass of Roncevaux? Whenever we grow too literal-minded about Menelaos and Diomede or the Trojans and their Thraco-Mysian-Phrygian allies, let us remember the Saracens of the Song of Roland and the death in a petty scrimmage of Hruodland, margrave of the March of Brittany.

There is, of course, nothing surprising in such deformation of history in the interests of poetry, where the literary and artistic appeal must dominate, character must be built and displayed, incident dramatically assembled into plot, and a coherent pattern imposed.

With a generous lapse of time, through the minds of successive generations of poets every epic must inevitably depart widely from its original factual source, not merely because human memory is fallible but also because human art is an active and formative power. A chronicle carved on palace or temple wall, if legible at all after long centuries, still presents the same record of events. Had its contents been retailed from mouth to mouth through those same centuries, the outcome would have been startlingly different. Indeed, just because error has no way of correcting itself where there is no written memorial and hence grows cumulatively more outrageous, the historic ignorance of the illiterate may verge on the incredible. Remarks a writer in discussing Mohammed's apparently oral composition of his Koran, "One would suppose that the most ignorant Jew could never have . . . identified Miriam, the sister of Moses, with Mariam, the mother of Christ," and concludes that such gross mistakes are due to "misconceptions such as only a listener (not the reader of a book) could fall into."

Similarly, the dramatic interest for a picturesque character will be stronger than any restraint of historic fact. The human mind is a stage on which all that it remembers may appear. In the Nibelungenlied, Etzel and Dietrich of Bern both occur. Dietrich clearly is dwelling in the land of the Huns, where Etzel is king; and at the very end of the poem both weep together over the slaughter. Now, Etzel is certainly Attila, king of the Huns, and Dietrich of Bern is no less surely the Ostrogoth Theodoric of Verona. Yet from the written Latin chronicles we are persuaded that Attila died on the night of his wedding with Ildico in A.D. 453, while Theodoric is with equal authority known not to have been born until the following year, 454; thus in actual fact they were never contemporaries at all.

Chronicle must keep to its count of the years, whereas oral literature in the long perspective of its tradition need not have the least compunction in blending into a single story any material, however chronologically disunited. Out of the poet's and storyteller's mind, like marionettes out of a chest, come all the wonderful people of the past, to play their parts in the same performance. Actual events are loosened from their proper time and place and held in the free suspension of the epic vision. Across their floating scenes may drift still other characters who never lived in this world at all, but have been lured from the secret domain whose primal law is wonder and magic. In the Lohengrin legend the knight of the swan drifts out of fairyland down the river Rhine to reach a real town and visit real people. And in the Nibelungenlied there consorts with Burgundians and Huns the heroic figure of Siegfried, whose identification with any historical character of the Latin chronicles can at best account for only the little in him which is Burgundian.

Equally illuminating are the historical references to be discovered in the Early English epic of Beowulf, wherein the English dialect and Northumbrian local color and appeal to Christian piety only lightly disguise the Danish and Swedish setting of its plot. Grendel and his evil dam, the dragon guarding the barrow, we shall do better not to claim for history. But the royal dynasties and genealogies of Geats and Danes are said to be proved accurate by the Scandinavian material available for control. In particular, Beowulf's uncle Hygelac and the Rhine-mouth raid in which Beowulf accompanied him and in which he (Hygelac) perished, are attested in the chronicle of Gregory of Tours and substantiated in the curious treatise called the *Liber Monstrorum*. What is more surprising is that in this verifiable environment of genuine persons and places there should move a hero whose name of "Bee-wolf" will not alliterate (as it should) with the names in the dynasty to which he is ascribed, and whose fantastically superhuman adventures and exploits can be made to yield a pattern comparable to that of the widely known and widely loved and utterly imaginary folk tale of The Bearson.

For the Homeric scholar the significant lesson is the remarkable homogeneity with which so much unrelated material has been fused and a vivid illusion of historical actuality produced by incorporating actual events and actual names of persons and places. And lest this lesson pass us by, we must mark that these are not accidental traits of the Lay of Beowulf or the Nibelungenlied or any other special brand of medieval poetry, but are standard components of popular epic, of which the Greek heroic epic is a specific but in no sense peculiar or abnormal species.

Let it be granted, willingly, that analogies from the epics of other races and epochs are not arguments leading to unarguable conclusions about the Homeric poems. But we should concede enough to them as parallels to entertain without further misgiving the hypothesis that to these Greek creations, also, historic oral tradition (saga), folk tale, fairy lore, and fancy may all have contributed, and that a specious unity of time and place (the time being heroic and Mycenaean, the place being for the most part the familiar land and sea of Greece) may be merely the mark of the storyteller's fictional skill in the practice of his ancient, honorable, and highly sophisticated profession.

CHAPTER III

TROUBLE OVER TROY

LONG AFTER *Treasure Island* had entered on a merited immortality, Robert Louis Stevenson cast his eyes back to the writing of his first book and made a little preface for it. Therein he indicated how an imaginary map of an imaginary island had been the chief factor in his plot, and proceeded to make merry over the topographical blunders of Walter Scott which he blamed on that writer's failure to equip himself with the essential cartographic insurance. "It is my contention," he wrote, "—my superstition, if you like—that he who is faithful to his map, and consults it, and draws from it his inspiration, daily and hourly, gains positive support, and not mere negative immunity from accident. The tale has a root there; it grows in that soil; it has a spine of its own behind the words.... The author must know his countryside, whether real or imaginary, like his hand; the distances, the points of the compass, the place of the sun's rising, the behaviour of the moon, should all be beyond cavil.... Better if the country be real, and he has walked every foot of it and knows every milestone."

If we apply this wisdom to our study of Homer, we must of course make the slight correction that, since there were no maps in those preliterate days, only an actual countryside, intimately familiar, could guarantee that freedom from internal contradiction which Stevenson calls "negative immunity from accident." If we walk the Trojan plain with printed Iliad in hand and find no puzzle or problem to resolve, but only a heightened clarity of comprehension of Homer's narrative, we shall have to conclude that Homer too had been there before us. And *per contra* if we are already convinced that the author of the Iliad had himself seen the Scamander plain in parched aridity and sudden flood, with its steep-cut banks lined with tamarisk and willow and elm, had seen Mount Ida carpeted with its glowing springtime flora, and all the landmarks of movement and battle which his poem records, then we are entitled to expect that there will be no topographic problems or contradictions.

Until Schliemann dug the *tell* of Hissarlik, this seemed indeed to be the case.

At the head of the alluvial plain formed by the Scamander, just where it breaks from a deep gorge in the western foothills of Mount Ida, there is a site occupied by the Turkish village of Bunarbashi, which takes its modern name from a set of perennial springs near by. A road leads to these springs, and here the women of Bunarbashi do their washing. The French scholar Pierron wrote in his 1869 edition of the Iliad:

> Nicolaides recounts that one may see the women of Bunarbashi washing their linen in troughs of marble or grayish stone close to the springs. The highroad of which he speaks is still passable today and the washbasins which he describes have not changed their function.

From Pierron back to Nicolaides is but a small step. Let us make the vastly greater stride and listen to the poet of the Iliad:

> And they sped beneath the wall along the wagon-road and came to two fair-flowing springs . . . and there beside them are broad fair washing-troughs of stone anigh, where the wives and fair daughters of the Trojans were wont to wash their shining clothes, in peacetime before the sons of the Achaians came.

Most of the fringe of the Scamander plain is arid and waterless; but at Bunarbashi, as its name implies, there is water running in abundance. The clear, cold, subsoil water breaks out in a number of perennial springs—so many that the Turks apply their favorite figure of uncounted multiplicity, *kirk,* which should mean "forty." Such prodigality is embarrassing; for the Iliad speaks specifically of two springs only:

And there twain fountains of eddying Scamander gush forth. And one flows with warmish water, and steam rises from it like smoke from burning fire; whereas the other in summer runs like unto hail or chill snow or the ice of water.

This betokens so unique a natural phenomenon that it should be easy to locate Homer's Troy merely by finding these two contrasted springs. Hence, it is hardly surprising that for the last two hundred years Anatolian travelers have been plunging thermometers into the Bunarbashi springs (as well as every other discoverable source for Scamander's stream) and wrangling over their findings. Had they pondered the text more carefully and known something of the unchanging peasant Greek mentality about water, they would have realized that, whether there be one spring or two or forty, the contrast is not between individual fountains but between the condition of their water in winter and in summer; for Homer does not speak of the water of one of the springs as hot or boiling, but quite specifically as *tepid* (λιαρόν), and a tepid spring would steam only in the coldest weather of *winter,* while it is the *summer* chill of the other which is specifically mentioned. Abundant water from the deep veins of a mountainside will hold its temperature the year round, so that it is cold when all the countryside is hot, yet seems warm when winter chill surrounds it. On frosty mornings it will even show vapor. Says the same source, Nicolaides, of the springs of Bunarbashi: "During summer the water of these springs is extremely cool; in winter, on the contrary, on really cold days, they are covered with steam, as though the water were boiling." I have myself heard modern peasants in various sections of Greece extol these identical properties as extraordinary virtues of some favorite spring. And Herodotos, without thought of Homer, describing the Fountain of the Sun in North Africa, speaks wonderingly of its apparent change of temperature in diametrical opposition to the waxing and waning of the day's heat. Thus the famous passage in the Iliad, in despite of its traditional and authoritative wording, bids us search not for a miraculous coupling of a warm geyser with an icy jet, but for some perennial deep-soil waterhead, tributary to the Scamander. And since this exists nowhere else in the Trojan plain except at Bunarbashi beneath the Bali Dag, and exists there to a degree spectacular for such a situation, Homer (to my thinking) has told us unequivocally and beyond argument where his imagination localized the legendary city of his poem. If that is so, we shall have high trouble over Troy.

The Bali Dag lies on the opposite side of the Scamander from the shore of the Hellespont, from which its slopes are invisible—two requirements for Troy which any unprejudiced reader of the Iliad will be able to deduce from the poem. With the entire river-plain available for battleground, it offers for the Trojan city a large and easily defensible area, protected by the deep gorge of the river and mounting to a conspicuous citadel nearly five hundred feet above the plain—a true Pergamos whither Apollo might retire to look "down and out" from his hilltop temple.

Such a site involves only one apparent discrepancy with the Troy which we must imagine for the Iliad. Since it is enclosed on two sides by the deep, winding gorge of the Scamander, no one could run or even walk around it; and who does not know that Achilles pursued the fleeing Hector thrice around the walls of Troy? It is strange that with all our high traditions of scholarship so erroneous an interpretation has persisted even among professional Homeric scholars. For it is a patent truth that in the Iliad neither Hector nor Achilles ever runs *around* Troy.

As when single-hooved horses contesting for prizes run full swiftly round the goals . . . so ran the twain with speedy feet three times about the town of Priam,

says the text. The comparison with horse racing is decisive, but presumably has evoked a faulty image in the modern mind, which perhaps visualizes Troy as a sort of central paddock around which the race is run. But if we go back to Greek and specifically to Homeric times we shall have to alter the picture. At the funeral games for Patroklos in the next to the last book of the Iliad a chariot race is described; and here the course runs straight to a fixed point and back over the selfsame track. This would, indeed, be the only picture possible to the minds of Homer and his audience. In Achilles' race in pursuit of Hector the two turning points are clearly stated. In one direction the goal is the Dardanian gate of Troy, where Hector hopes to dart beneath the protection of his townsmen's weapons showered from the walls. But Achilles closes in upon him and forces him out from beneath this shelter and thence along the road to the watering troughs at the washerwomen's springs; around these he darts as around the turning mark in a race. Knowing only the practice of racing up and back on a single track, the Greek mind would have instantly and correctly grasped the Homeric picture and not for a moment imagined Hector and Achilles encircling the entire town. True, the Greek text says "around the town," but only in the sense in which we too say that we have been driving "around town" without meaning that we have encircled it. The Greek preposition *peri* carries no circular halo.* And this leaves us with no further obstacle to our site for Homeric Troy except the one which seems to most scholars so completely decisive and to me largely irrelevant—the discovery by Schliemann of a prehistoric settlement on the mound of Hissarlik, five miles nearer the sea.

Before Schliemann dug, competent visitors to the Scamander

* So, for example, the Peripatetics are not the philosophers who walk in circles, but *up and down, to and fro,* as they discuss their problems. L. and S. correctly translate ἡ περὶ Λέσβον ναυμαχία, "the sea-fight *off* Lesbos"—an exact parallel to Achilles' pursuit of Hector περὶ ἄστυ. Cf. Il. XVII. 760 περί τ' ἀμφί τε τάφρον, where obviously one cannot fight in a circle around a straight line. So Od. IV. 368 περὶ νῆσον ἀλώμενοι should not be interpreted 'along the shore on a circular tour of the island,' but 'up and down,' 'criss-cross,' in every direction at random. Cf. also περιβαίνειν for riding *astride,* περίγειος of the moon when *nearest* the earth, and specifically περίδρομοι, the *laps* of a (rectilinear) race.

plain were in pretty general agreement that Homer's Troy lay on the Bali Dag above Bunarbashi. After Schliemann dug, opinion veered; in the end, the world came to accept Schliemann's site so decisively that those who still argue the matter are treated as perverse and contentious nuisances. Yet there are obvious indications* that Hissarlik does not agree with the situation demanded by the Iliad, which speaks of a great walled city with streets, houses, and palaces, rising to a temple-crowned acropolis, at an appreciable distance from the Hellespont and apparently invisible from it, situated across the Scamander, with abundant springs of deep-soil water gushing close at hand. Actually, Hissarlik is in plain sight of the Hellespont, on the same side of the river, without any running springs, and enclosed within its walls an area of less than five acres.

When confronted with these discrepancies, some of the Schliemannites ignore them or brush them aside—which is certainly the simplest and easiest and (if one can do so with tranquillity) most satisfactory way of dealing with them. But a very considerable group, aware of Homer's realistic sentiments and persuaded of the accurate and conscientious staging of his poem, admit the topographic problems to be serious and try to find some method of reconciling them with the actual terrain. The violence—one might almost say, impertinence—of some of these solutions is chiefly interesting as proving that there really is something amiss with the conventional identification of Hissarlik with Troy.

Nothing can be done to make a five-acre stronghold into a broad-streeted town with palaces and temples on a lofty acropolis; nor can Hissarlik be moved farther from the shore or made invisible from it; nor can the Bunarbashi springs be made to flow beneath its walls. But the embarrassment in finding Hissarlik on the same side of the Scamander as the Hellespontine beach has been dealt with in terms of extreme rigor. By some, the Scamander

* Persistently presented and examined with undeviating conviction by Charles Vellay in recent years.

has been made to seek a different bed from its present one: in Homer's time, it is averred, it used to run along the opposite rim of the Trojan plain. (Few competent investigators have considered this very probable!) Others, with even greater courage, have left the river but moved the Hellespont. Since these violent solutions seldom recommend themselves to any except their proponents, we are left with the uncomfortable suspicion that there is something wrong either with Schliemann's Troy or with Homer's, but that there is nothing much to be done about it. Yet there is something very simple to be done; and that is to examine the grounds for thinking that the identity of the poet's site for his city can be established by digging in the soil. For it is a thesis as truthful as it is simple, that Saga vivified by Fiction—by which we mean Homer's epic—belongs in a wholly different category from history reclaimed by archaeology.

The Schliemannites demand: "If Homer knew about Troy at all, how could he have failed to know where Troy was? Must not a local tradition (such as kept alive the memory of Mycenae and Tiryns in mainland Greece and some recollection of the Knossian 'labyrinth' in Crete) have attached itself to the conspicuous ruin-mound which the Romans had no difficulty in recognizing for Ilium when they came to refound a city of that name? Why should Homer arbitrarily have set local knowledge aside and invented a Troy of his own?"

He might have done so through ignorance or by deliberate design. Through ignorance, if it be considered that, unlike Schliemann, Homer did not dig. If perchance he was a Greek poet living in Greek times, what would he (or could he) have known of the invisible and largely destroyed contents of the bramble-grown and probably deserted hill which we call Hissarlik? But it is far more probable that the selection of a site for Troy on the spacious and commanding height of Bali Dag was deliberate, because by Homer's time the Troy saga had swollen to legendary size. And there is a still more cogent and compelling reason. Homer, who knew so little of the actualities of Mycenaean culture, was familiar with the classical *polis,* the town wherein all the townsmen dwelt together, and knew nothing of the preclassical feudal distinction between chieftain and commoners, which is reflected in the heavily protected castle surrounded by an undefended settlement at Mycenae and Tiryns. Hissarlik was a Helladic *Herrenburg,* or chieftain's castle, with room only for the ruling dynasty, whereas in Homer's conception (and therefore in the Iliad!) Troy was a Greek town with space enough for its entire population inside its own walls. By the time he had imagined for his poem a palace with "fifty chambers of polished stone" for Priam's married sons, "and for his daughters twelve roofed chambers" and "a chamber and hall and courtyard" for Paris hard by those of Hector and Priam the king, and a temple for Athena and another for Apollo, and broad streets between houses sufficient for several thousand citizens with their families, he could not have put it all on Hissarlik if he had wanted to, no matter what the local inhabitants said! One can do a great deal with a five-acre lot; but there are limits beyond which even a poet cannot go.

But what if a classical contemporary who visited the Scamander could find no traces of Troy's high gates and walls where the poem seemed to demand them, on the barren Bali Dag? The same poetic conscience which had betrayed its qualms over the moated wall across the plain—the wall which, because it had never existed in actual fact, had to be obliterated by all the floods of Ida and the sea—could easily create the face-saving epic tradition (of which we specifically hear)* that, when at last the Greeks captured Troy, they left not one stone upon another but removed every trace of that proud (and wholly legendary) site.

* E.g., Euripides, *Helen* 108, ὥστ' οὐδ' ἴχνος γε τειχέων εἶναι σαφές ("that not a single certain trace of walls remain") could hardly have been said by a Greek who claimed Hissarlik for the site of the Homeric city.

But what of the projecting fragments of walls on Hissarlik? Homer must somehow have worked these into his poem's topography. With so much conscientious realism, extending even to the ancient barrows of heaped earth which here and there marked the district, landmarks which Homer knows by name—the "grave of Aisyetes," the "steep hillock before the town, in the plain apart, to be passed on either side,* which men call Batieia, but the immortals the tomb of skipping Myrina"—he could scarcely have left this greater mound unmentioned. Perhaps he gave it its legendary due in the twentieth book when he told how

the black-haired god led the way to the *high tumbled wall of Herakles* which the Trojans under Pallas Athena built for him that he might escape to safety from the sea-monster when it pursued him landward from the beach.

Like the pulpits and bridges which a more modern European peasantry ascribes to the devil, the vestiges of a preclassical fortress could become a "Wall of Herakles" to the Greek inhabitants of the Scamander plain.

"But surely," it will be objected, "one could not thus move around at will a famous legendary site!" Whoever holds that Homer was taking atrocious liberties in picking a site to his own liking, some five miles farther upriver toward Mount Ida,†

* *περίδρομος ἔνθα καὶ ἔνθα* is an excellent instance of what *περί* meant to a Greek. The phrase certainly did not mean that one could make the complete circuit of the hill both clockwise and counterclockwise!

† A location for Homer's Troy stoutly championed by Demetrios of Skepsis, who estimated the distance, however, at *four* miles. Modern commentators of Strabo's jumbled report on Demetrios' thesis have made confusion worse confounded by failing to realize that the transference of Homer's Troy from the Bali Dag to Hissarlik inevitably involved a change in identification for the Simoeis, so as to keep it close to Troy. For Homer, the Simoeis was the modern Kemer Su; for the Hissarlik-Ilium school, it had to be the Dumbrek Su, whose modern name shows that in spite of learned and official argument it continued to cling to its old proper name as the 'river of Thymbra' (or Dumbra, *Hesych.*), i.e., the *Thymbrikos* or *Dumbrikos*. It is here in the lateral valley above Hissarlik that Rhesos and his Thracians were encamped in the Doloneia. The Simoeis, on the other hand, which "joined its stream" with Scamander and to which the Scamander appealed for added flood with which to drown Achilles, lay opposite the Bali Dag and had its confluence with the Scamander just after that river had emerged from the great gorge.

should look more closely still at the name of Troy. For it seems to have only an epic sanction and no historical or geographical actuality whatever.

In the Iliad, Troy is so infrequently used as the name of the city (which is called Ilios) as to make it probable that it was traditionally not the title of a town at all, but of a district or region—of whatever land may have been inhabited by the Trojans. But there do not seem to have been any Trojans except in the city of Ilios. Certainly, in historic Greek times no Trojans survived in Asia Minor, or anywhere else. They had vanished as completely as Achilles' Myrmidons. Apparently there were *Ilians* still alive in Hellenistic days, because Polybios mentions them and Demetrios of Skepsis identified Troy with a "settlement of the Ilians" extant in his time. But there were no Trojans. And Greek geographers continually quarreled over the boundaries of the Troad, for the sufficient reason that the term was unreal and without content for them, there being no Trojans anywhere nor any towns or districts, rivers or mountains, known to have belonged to them.

One would imagine that some epic tradition of great antiquity and authority must have vouched for Troy's identity with Ilios and thus fixed its site close to the Hellespont. But there was a well-supported and very astonishing countertradition at complete variance with such a supposition.

The lost epic called the Cypria, whose contents are barely known to us through a Byzantine digest of a late-classical prose summary, related the causes and beginnings of the Trojan War—the judgment of Paris and the rape of Helen from Sparta, the gathering of the Greek forces at Aulis, and the incident of the snake devouring the sparrows which every schoolboy remembers. But then comes the surprise: the expedition puts to sea and "touches at Teuthrania, and this they plunder in mistake for Ilion."

Could anything be more preposterous or less credible?

Paris has abducted Helen and kept her some two hundred miles away on the other shore of an easily navigable sea. Throughout mainland Greece, great preparations are made for her recovery and a formidable force gathers. Yet when the expedition descends upon the Asiatic shore and joins in bloody fray with the natives, the discovery is made that there has been an error in the objective, the attack has been directed against the wrong people! Paris and Helen are not here; this is not Ilion at all; this is Mysian Teuthrania! Up sails, out oars, then, and away again in search of the proper Troy! But now a sudden storm scatters the fleet, which never reaches the Hellespont. Achilles finds himself in the little rocky isle of Skyros and seems content to abandon the campaign, since he marries the local princess. As for the vengeance on Helen's lover, all must be begun anew. Once more the heroes are summoned; once more they gather at Aulis; once again there are difficulties at the sacrifices for a fair sailing, with the same soothsayer Kalchas expounding prophetically the same portent of snake and sparrows. Now at last they sail. They have learned by this time where Troy is; they steer, this second time, for Tenedos and force a landing at the Hellespont. The siege of the true Troy is on.

It is obvious that such a story merely repeats itself. Everything happens twice with hardly so much as a shift of scene or setting. But this is not all. From other fragmentary accounts and allusions, ranging from Pindar to Pausanias, Quintus Smyrnaeus, and scholia on the Iliad, we can piece together something more of the lost tradition about this earlier and wretchedly mistaken expedition against Troy. It seems that (precisely as happens in the Iliad) the Greeks after landing were driven back to their ships, that Patroklos came to the rescue and repulsed the enemy, but in the encounter was wounded, thereby motivating the intervention of Achilles who (as in the Iliad) singled out and pursued the native champion (in the Iliad, Hector; here, Telephos). Here too he was unable, for all his swiftness of foot, to overtake his fleeing adversary until a divine stratagem was contrived. In the Iliad, Athena assumes the likeness of the Trojan Deiphobos and in this guise persuades Hector to take his stand against Achilles, then promptly vanishes, leaving her dupe to face his destroyer alone. In the Teuthranian version, Dionysos magically causes a vine to spring and trip the fleeing Telephos, so that Achilles can overtake and sorely wound him. Thereafter Achilles returns to Patroklos, and the decision to depart is taken; but as the fleet sets sail, a storm overtakes and scatters it, just as in the tale of Troy the victorious Greeks are caught by a tempest and scattered abroad as they seek to return to their homes.

And there are also such subtly hidden and apparently unsuspected doublets as that of the wounded Telephos who must be healed by the weapon which smote him, since he is fated to show the way to Troy, to be compared with Philoktetes bitten by a serpent and abandoned on the island of Lemnos, who must be brought to Troy and healed for sake of his weapons before the city can fall.

From such far-reaching duplication it is obvious that the two versions are at bottom so alike precisely because they were not two stories, but one and the same story told of two different places. And Telephos has at least as much right to be at home in Teuthrania as Hector in Ilios. In short, the great expedition may not have made so utterly silly a mistake: for some tellers of the story Teuthrania and not Ilios may in truth have been Troy.

For this hypothesis there are several confirmatory bits of evidence. For instance, there is the Oxyrhynchus papyrus (xi. 1359) which preserves a fragment of some epic of the Hesiodic School, setting the birth of Telephos at Troy; but as Telephos cannot be uprooted from Teuthranian Pergamon, then Pergamon for this poet must have been Troy. This same Pergamon may be an intruder into Homer's Troy, where it serves to designate the highest quarter of the town, where the temples stand, whereas in Teuthrania it is a place name in its own right, marking a conspicuous rocky ridge above the river Kaikos, some fifteen miles from its mouth, well suited to play the role of Troy for this broad river valley above the Aegean beaches. If in the Iliad the town where Helen is held captive is called rather indiscriminately Troy, Ilios, and Pergamos, and the river on which the town walls front is called indifferently Xanthos and Scamander, we may detect in this superfluity of names the vicissitudes of a legend in which traditional, and hence already legendary, names have been tied by poets to the actual geography of their own world, one school (shall we call it the Aeolic?) attaching Troy and its river to Teuthrania at Pergamon above the Kaikos, the other (shall we call it the Ionic?) to the Hellespont at Ilios on the Scamander. In addition to Pergamos, the Iliad seems to have borrowed two other place names from the Teuthranian version. Myrina (which in the Iliad is used of a burial mound with an alternate and perhaps correct local name of Batieia) was an actual place name in Teuthrania for an Aeolic town opposite the Kaikos mouth; near by to the south, at Kyme, there flowed an actual river Xanthos. And much of the incidental warfare of foraying and raiding, to which the Iliad makes considerable reference, likewise indicates that the Achaean expedition had been occupying itself with a different countryside and was not really based on the Dardanelles. Agamemnon makes mention of a sacking of Lesbos; and since the Odyssey speaks of the island as a way station for the Greek forces returning from Troy, the Greek occupation was apparently permanent. Opposite Lesbos, at the head of the Adramyttian Gulf, lay "Thebe-beneath-Mount-Plakos," of which Achilles is made to say, "We sacked it thoroughly and carried everything away." It was here that Hector's wife Andromache was born, and here that Achilles slew her father Eetion, the ruler of the town. Thence also he took the lyre with which he later consoled himself while he sulked inactive before Troy. Near at hand—or presumably so, since it was inhabited by the same people—lay Lyrnessos. It was from the sack of this town that Achilles had acquired the maiden Briseis, at whose loss (as everyone knows) the wrath of Achilles was aroused. Not far away—since it is mentioned in the same verse with Lyrnessos—lay Pedasos, another prize of war captured by Achilles. Then there are the raids in the vales of Mount Ida, far inland from Ilios, but close to the Lesbian gulf, where Achilles plundered the cattle of Aeneas and drove him a fugitive into Lyrnessos. In summary of all this petty warring, so unrelated to the major task of taking Troy and recapturing Helen, Achilles boasts,

> And thus I bivouacked many nights unsleeping
> And bloody days fulfilled in constant battle,
> Striving with men for sake of these men's women.
> Twelve were the towns which with my ships I plundered,
> Eleven took afoot in Troy's rich country.

But so far as any of these twenty-three towns are specified, they all lay on the southern slopes of Mount Ida or in the level land to the south, which adjoins Teuthrania. Now, this shoreland was the zone of the Aeolic penetration and colonization of Asia Minor, based on the island of Lesbos and spreading naturally to the mainland visible immediately opposite. So that Achilles' plundering of mainland cattle and sacking of the little towns near the sea has often been held to be a direct reflection, a folk memory kept by the poets, of a none-too-peaceful Aeolic settlement; and to this same movement the attack on the "false Troy" of Teuthrania would belong. The date of this Aeolic migration is very uncertain; but classical Greek tradition and modern scholarship alike assign it to a later phase of Greek history than the heroic age of Mycenae. If the legend of the Achaean expedition against Troy is Mycenaean, it has been obscured and contaminated by later Aeolic history in the telling. Yet, since the record of these Aeolic quarrels survives in the Iliad in spite of their inappropriateness to the siege of Hellespontine Troy, we shall have to conclude that the Aeolic version (however belated from a Mycenaean point of view) is earlier than the Ionic and that the "false Troy" of Teuthrania can claim priority over the "true Troy" of Homer.

Shall we say that it was Homer who brought Troy to the Dardanelles?

It would be more prudent not to insist that the Iliad was the first to make the identification. Rather, let us credit it to the Ionic school of epic, which inherited so much else from the Aeolic and so often transmuted it into its own Ionic terms. The Hellespont was the highway of *Ionic* penetration eastward even before the great commercial expansion of Miletus in the seventh century B.C.;* and if along the Hellespont, where so many an Ionic ship eastward bound must have touched shore, some Ionic poet discovered a local tradition in the lower Scamander plain of an ancient stronghold sacked and burned in the long-distant past, he might well believe (or choose to assert) that here was the Troy of legend.

What then is left of our Trojan story, if we cannot locate the true Troy of saga either on Hissarlik or on the Bali Dag? We shall have to eliminate as fictitious most of the play of battle, all the local topographic color, the epic tropes and commonplaces, the chivalresque ornament and incident. Drastic as this is, it does

* There is no archaeological evidence for anything but the most superficial penetration of the Black Sea basin by the Mycenaean culture. After the Mycenaean collapse, the intervening Sea of Marmora should have been reached and exploited very early in the commercial expansion of the Ionians of the Asia Minor coast, who would have followed the "fish track" of the Hellespont for sake of the rich hauls of tunny. But there was at first nothing whatever to attract them further, into the inhospitable Black Sea, until the breakdown of land communications with the Anatolian metal lands, due primarily to the Cimmerian irruption *ca.* 700 B.C., prompted them to establish a seaway to the "birthland of silver." It follows that the Tale of the Argonauts could not have been localized as a journey through the Bosporos all the way to the Caucasian shoreland of the Black Sea much before the middle of the seventh century.

not leave us entirely empty-handed. There remains the insistent tradition that the man power of heroic Greece gathered and took to the sea for a great and distant exploit, that it landed on a hostile coast where it maintained a precarious hold against obstinate resistance, that an alliance of native forces set fire to its ships, that (perhaps) plague decimated its numbers, that the success of its efforts was at least so doubtful that in the end, instead of establishing their power and holding the hostile land by conquest, the invaders took to their remaining ships and dispersed, and that disastrously few of the original band ever returned to their native land. Shall we say that this, the persistent and irreducible minimum of the Troy legend, must be true?

If there is one conclusion that stands firm in the study of medieval epic legend as it occurs in such poems as the Nibelungenlied, the Song of Roland, Beowulf, and their kind, it is that one and all are dependent on actual incident and historic fact for some of their material, but that they present to the analyst an irreversible process. If he already knows the history from other sources (such as contemporary prose chronicles), he can discover how events have been distorted and transmuted to suit the irresponsible humors of the poets; but if, on the contrary, he knows only the epics, he can never hope to change them back into the history out of which they arose. Presumably, therefore, for want of written records from the crucial centuries preceding those of the classical Greek culture, we shall never know what or where was Troy.

But if we care to indulge in speculation on actual historical events which *might* have been responsible for the saga tradition out of which ultimately emerged the legend of the Trojan War, there are two possibilities which deserve consideration, even if they can never pass beyond the twilight zone of pure hypothesis.

For a first suggestion we may follow the hint of the persistent Greek suspicion that Helen never went to Hellespontine Troy, but passed the years of the war securely on the Nile. The Odyssey knows of Menelaos and Helen together in Egypt after the fall of Troy; Stesichoros in his famous palinode asserted that Helen had been there "for the duration"; Herodotos could give the details of the story and suspected that Homer must have been familiar with it but "discarded it because it was not as suitable for his poem as the version which he used"; and both the Iliad and the Cypria point in the same direction by making Paris touch at Sidon in Phoenicia on his way home from Sparta with abducted Helen. Sidon does not lie between Cape Malea and the Dardanelles. Finally, Euripides gave the legend dramatic form and authority in his tragedy called *Helen*. And let us note (for what it is worth) that Odysseus in his yarn to the swineherd also claimed that he had voyaged to Egypt and remained there seven years, gathering riches. A trend so contradictory to Homer's official version could scarcely have maintained itself in full classical times except by the vitality of old authority. Somewhere in the saga, it would seem, there lurked a memory of a heroic expedition which had had Egypt for its goal.

On the walls of the temple at Medinet Habu in Egypt is a series of reliefs depicting a great naval battle in which the forces of "the northern countries . . . who came from their lands in the islands in the midst of the sea" (as the accompanying hieroglyphic text declares) are being annihilated by the navy of Rameses III. The date is about 1190 B.C., almost precisely the year of the sack of Troy according to one of the most widely favored classical computations of that distant event. The often-quoted account in the Egyptian record may bear one more repetition here:

> The Isles were restless, disturbed among themselves. No land stood before them, not Kheta nor Kadi, Karchemish, Arvad, or Alashiya. They destroyed them: they assembled their camp in the midst of Amor: they came with fire prepared before them, forward towards Egypt.

I caused the Nile mouths to be prepared like a strong wall with warships, galleys, and coasting-vessels.... As for those who advanced together on the sea ... a net was prepared to ensnare them.... At the Nile mouths the full flame was in front of them, a stockade of lances surrounded them on the shore: they were dragged, hemmed in, laid low on the beach, slain, made into heaps: their ships and their goods were as if fallen into the sea.

Piecing the records together, within a few years of each other there were "Achaiwa-sha" (who should be "Achaiwoi" or Achaeans) and "Denyuna" (who sound like Danaoi), northerners, from the isles in the sea (which can hardly be anything but the Aegean), attempting a great naval raid on the rich land of Egypt, coming to grief with their land armies shattered and their ships destroyed, and thereafter apparently scattering abroad (mainly along the Palestinian coast) rather than attempting to retrace their path home. With them, and with this great but unsuccessful attack on Egypt, the Mycenaean empire seems to have dissolved.

Obviously, this event coincides surprisingly closely with the essential nucleus of the heroic legend of the expedition to Troy, where in a mighty concerted effort the Greek peoples which called themselves Argives, Danaans, and Achaeans gathered their forces, took to their ships, fought desperately (and perhaps disastrously) to capture a locality which they knew as Troy, and were scattered far and wide in the sequel, some finding their way home to Greece, many never returning but settling abroad. So widespread was the exodus that, judging from the dearth of legend about the immediately succeeding years, Greece remained depleted and its civilization in decadence or collapse. With the sailing of the great armada the Heroic Age approached its end.

True, the Egyptian texts chronicle the utter defeat of the northern invaders, while Greek saga insists that Troy was conquered and destroyed. But this would by no means be the only instance of the legendary conversion of a great national disaster into a pretended victory. No one reading the Nibelungenlied with its Burgundian victory over the Huns would suspect (what Prosper of Aquitaine records in his contemporary chronicle) that in the year 437 it was the Burgundian king who with all his followers was destroyed by a raiding band of Huns. With such an instance in mind, whoever attentively reviews the Troy legend—the repeated suggestion of the Achaean leaders that they had better pull out and sail for home, the prolonged failure of the siege, the desperate straits of the Greeks when fire was set to their ships, the failure of so many of the heroes ever to return, the downfall of the great dynasties shortly after—may harbor legitimate suspicion whether all went as well for the Greeks before Troy as the epic version of the story maintained.

Though it may have contributed its share to the formation of the Troy saga, the great Achaean raid on Egypt cannot be held responsible for the entire legend, because it leaves the name of Troy completely unexplained. "Ilios" we took to be a name at home on the lower Scamander, where Demetrios of Skepsis still knew a "village of the Ilians" and, before him, Homer had known a tomb mound of Ilos, "the old Dardanid." "Pergamos" we took to be a borrowing from the "false" Troy on the Kaikos. But "Troia" has eluded us. Etymologically it seems completely obscure, which is in favor of its authenticity, since it cannot be dismissed as a transparent Greek invention. Linguistically the word is in an unstable and transitional stage in Homer, being trisyllabic and hence indicating a recent loss between the "o" and the "i," suggestive of some such original form as *TROVIA or *TROSIA. If the latter, then the equation with Latin E-TRURIA—as that of TRŌS with T(R)US-CUS—is philologically unobjectionable, though rather startling in its implications.

So flimsy an etymological bridge perhaps does not deserve to be crossed. Yet a halfhearted theory is no theory at all; and every hypothesis (if only in test of its folly) should be thought out to its final conclusions. If the Trojans were the oral-epic counterparts of the historic Etruscans, the conquest of their Asiatic homeland by a Greek invasion would mean that it was the Greeks (most probably in the course of the Aeolic migration) who drove them out and thus were responsible for the initial Etruscan migration to Italy. We have already seen reason for seriously considering the claims of the "false" (or Aeolic) Troy of Pergamon-Teuthrania in preference to the Homeric (or Ionic) Troy at the Hellespont. It may therefore be significant that so highly competent a student of the intricate problem of Etruscan origins as Schachermeyer, in his *Etruskische Frühgeschichte,* reached the conclusion not merely that the Etruscans came from Asia Minor, but that their most probable place of origin was precisely northwestern Asia Minor in the region around Teuthrania. Nor is it perhaps without significance that Vergil, aware that Aeneas was no denizen of the Hellespont, makes his hero after the fall of Troy retire to his own Dardanian land under Ida and there, at Antandros on the Adramyttian Gulf, build the ships in which his people are to set out for Italy. And no sooner are they arrived in Italy than Aeneas allies himself with the Etruscans and unites their forces with his in a joint occupation of Latium. So also Alkiphron, that weaver of difficult riddles, must have had some prior warrant for accounting Tyrsenos and Tarchon (patent eponyms of the Etruscan people) to be sons of none other than *Telephos* (the king of Mysian Troy). And, as far as we can set dates to such elusive happenings, the movement of the Etruscans toward Italy synchronizes well enough with the Aeolic Greek penetration of Asia Minor.

Such a far-reaching and temerarious inference from nothing more than a suppositious identity of a verbal root may be poor historical method, but it at least gives us a hypothesis with which to explain three things which have for long sorely puzzled the experts. First, it would explain why Latin national tradition was so insistent that there had been an early *Trojan* immigration to Latium, when archaeology can establish only an *Etruscan* penetration; secondly, it would explain why the Trojans seem to have vanished without trail, track, or sign from the horizon of Greek historic memory; and thirdly, it would explain why the Tyrrhenians and their kinsmen, the Asia Minor ancestors of the Etruscans, are so consistently ignored by Greek epic, which mentions the Etruscan name only in a single notice in Hesiod and relegates the Tyrrhenians to a Homeric hymn of unknown antiquity. Actually, the Trojan stock and speech would have survived in the Tyrrhenian folk of the northeast-Aegean islands of Lemnos and Imbros and (probably) Samothrace, where as late as the fifth century B.C. there were inhabitants who still spoke, and knew how to write in Greek letters, an un-Greek language. And Greek epic would have done the very opposite of turning its back in total obliviousness on the Asiatic Etruscans and their westward migration if it was in truth these who had supplied the central historic event for its celebrated Sack of Troy.

Granted that the Etruscan migration to Italy did not occur in Mycenaean times nor had any connection with the Atreid dynasty of Mycenae or the Achaean raid on Egypt, it still would have been entirely possible for two completely unrelated series of events, as much as two hundred years apart, to have become fused and identified in popular memory. The Achaean armada in Egypt with its disastrous sequel for heroic Greece, and the Aeolic displacement of the Etruscan Tyrrhenians of Mysia with its apparent disaster for the emigrant Tyrrhenians, could have been joined into a single story. It is easy for oral epic thus to project its themes against the flat screen of an almost timeless past. In medieval German poetry Ermanrich from the fourth century, Attila from the fifth, and Theodoric from the sixth all appear contemporaneously, to be joined by Siegfried, who may be immeasurably older than any of them. Why should the Iliad have any greater compunction in introducing characters from the Achaean age, such as Agamemnon, Menelaos, or Nestor, along with others from some period of Aeolic-Tyrrhenian conflict, and bring them all into intimacy with a fairy-tale hero such as Achilles, whose unmatchable prowess is proof that his youthfulness was of that unaging variety which is as old as the wistfulness of mankind? For of such materials are oral epics made.

These would not be the only contaminations and conflations to be detected or suspected in the Iliad. Some of the minor folk at Troy (such as Theanô who kept the keys to Athena's temple on the acropolis) are Thracian; and various scholars have held that Priam and Paris are Thracian names. Yet, since the Thraco-Phrygian invasions almost certainly succeeded the period of Mycenaean glory, these may be anachronisms as serious as the Phrygian cap which classical art was fond of giving Paris. And what is Memnon the Ethiopian prince, son of the dawn, doing as a Trojan ally, when (as later Greek criticism saw) he ought to be an Egyptian pharaoh? or Penthesileia, the Thracian Amazon? Yet both appeared at Troy, if not in the verses of the Iliad. Or, reverting to the Iliad itself, how could there have been Cilicians (who belong around Tarsus on the coast this side of Syria) living at "Thebe-under-Plakos" within raiding distance of Troy? Yet Hector's Andromache had been a princess in Thebe and was presumably a Cilician. And is it plausible that among the Trojan allies there should figure prominently warriors from the aloof mountain-locked land of Lycia, especially in view of the connection, familiar to Homer and stressed in the Bellerophon story, between the Lycian dynasty and a Mycenaean royal house in mainland Greece? So strange is it that these Lycian princes should turn up at the distant Dardanelles to fight against their own Argive kindred that Homer himself cannot quite brook it, but checks them on the very brink of combat in that delightful incident wherein Glaukos and Diomede hold up the entire fearful fray while the Lycian explains who he is and the Greek refuses to fight with an old family friend.

And so all manner of unrelated material finally comes together under the collective focus of the epic vision. Pre-Hellenic Hissarlik—so its most recent excavators assure us—was twice destroyed in the Helladic epoch, once by earthquake and once by Thracians (or similar northern invaders) from the Danube; but no evidence has been found for any destruction at the hands of Greek mainlanders. How should there be such evidence if Troy (by any chance) was really the name of the Etruscan homeland in Aeolis and the naval expedition which brought the Mycenaean empire to ruin actually spent itself far away at the mouth of the Nile? History is history, and oral epic is oral epic: we shall gain nothing by mistaking the one for the other.

CHAPTER IV

FOLK TALE AND FICTION IN THE ILIAD

IT IS A PITY that we have no convenient English word to designate fairy tales with no fairies in them. Folk tale, the term which we have been constrained to use, may apply to any story of popular tradition and popular appeal, as distinguished from literary creations by self-conscious authors. But there are many stories to be classed in this category which yet do not concern our inquiry. Some make their point by humor. Others are brief tales of character and situation—miniature *novelle*. Our interest centers in a more restricted and specialized type, for which there is no better word than the German *Märchen*. Our common nursery fairy stories mostly belong to this type; but the presence of fairy folk is not essential to them. Rather, their distinctive characteristic is the appeal to magic and the use of specific patterns formed on fundamental human desires and fears. Cinderella, Snow-white, Puss-in-boots, Jack the Giant-killer are good familiar examples. Many of these must be of high antiquity. If we distinguish—as professional students of *Märchen* insist that we must—between *Märchen* motifs or formulas on the one hand and *Märchen* plots or story patterns on the other, we shall probably decide that many of the *motifs* are of world-wide recurrence and believe in their polygenesis, whereas the more highly organized composite *plots* may have a monogenetic origin. In this view of the situation, the material mechanism and the common stuff in which *Märchen* deals are drawn from universal human behavior, while the complex structure of the more developed stories demands an individual creator or group of fabricators. Fortunately, we do not need further to explore this extremely hazardous distinction; yet we must pause long enough to note its existence and consider its probable significance for Homeric epic.

An important ingredient in the immediately recognizable flavor of *Märchen* is the universal and deep-seated human delight in overcoming in the imagination the frustrations and physical barriers of ordinary earthly existence. It is this which engenders and keeps alive the appeal to the supernatural, the magical; it is this which endows the heroes of *Märchen* (who in the last analysis must of course be none other than you and I, the enthralled listeners) with speed beyond mere running, strength of arm and endurance beyond all fatigue, sight able to penetrate all obstacles, hearing beyond the human range of sound, comprehension of the song of birds and the speech of animals, power to forsake human shape and to take on the form of beasts or things more elemental, power to penetrate the sky and the sea and the hollow earth (even though the dead may dwell there), release from poverty and manual labor, with consequent acquisition of wealth and pomp and power, and for final attainment the hand of a king's daughter and a happy life forever after. The lowlier the victim and the bitterer the humiliations of frustration, the more stirring the release and the final triumph. Hence the typical hero of *Märchen* is the little tradesman, the runt of the family, the ne'er-do-well of the community, or—if everything must move on the golden plane—the youngest prince or the ugliest princess.

A second constituent of *Märchen* seems to be compounded of fear rather than desire, and specifically fear expressing itself in much the same form as shapes our dreams when we are asleep. Perhaps some of the favorite accomplishments of *Märchen,* such as the power of floating through air or of living under water, are dreamlike also. The man-eating ogres, the wild and violent giants, the horrors that dwell in forest, mountain, and water, all seem bred of secret fear and are probably not—as the anthropological explanation would persuade us—surviving memories of primitive cannibalism and precommunal life.

For all this yearning against frustration and escape from calamity the literary Greeks cared nothing. To them, the imaginary supernatural adventures of *Märchen* remained pointless and unattractive. The Greek did not desire to ignore or overstep human limitations so much as to master and control them. What his secret longings were, we may guess from the character of his Olympian gods and thence derive a simple catalogue of life's delectations—leisure for drinking and conversing, escape from old age and disease, freedom from the toil of amassing food and material wealth: in short, not a magic world, the antithesis of his own, but ordered communal existence rid of its hindrances and laborious inconveniences. All in all, I see little difference between the type of existence regretfully projected by the Greeks on the inaccessible height of Mount Olympus and our own modern aspirations projected with equal assurance on the rather more accessible peak of the highly mechanized technological future. Yet, in spite of his modern material-mindedness, because the classical Greek spoke a European language the European heritage of magic and *Märchen,* with its wistful and childish overleaping of earthly obstacles by mere daydreaming, must have reached him. But as a Hellene of the mother race of philosophers, mathematicians, and political realists, he refused this barbaric and uncivilized birthright, rejecting its supernatural excesses in favor of the reasonable human norm. Like the hybrid monsters of eastern imagination when they came under Greek artists' hands, the northern *Märchen* had to be re-formed and retold in more natural human terms before a Greek literary audience could accept them.

Most certainly, one may find fairy stories—*Märchen* plots and *Märchen* motifs—in Greek literature. Herodotos came close to showing a real sense for them when he recounted the tale of Rhampsinitos; but he showed his Hellenic (or was it merely his Levantine?) bias by extolling craft and trickery over wizardry and marvel. In consequence, his *Märchen* turned out to be a *novella.* Plato touched on a similar domain in his story of Gyges' ring, but converted the fairy tale into moral allegory. Near the very end of Greek literary history, Lucian rescued the flotsam and jetsam of *Märchen* in eastern Greco-Roman keeping, but only to hold it up to the sophisticated ridicule of a fancied intellectual superiority. In Homer, despite the obvious opportunity, *Märchen* is heavily disguised or deliberately converted. The ships of the Phaiakians, which travel with the speed of thought and without the aid of human hands; Circe's drugs and wand which change men into beasts, and Hermes' herbal countermagic "which the gods call *moly"*; one-eyed Polyphemos, as tall as a mountain, with a tree for a walking stick; the loathsome queen of the Laestrygons, huge as a mountaintop; the king of the winds, who feasts on a floating island with his six sons wedded to his six daughters; the Sirens with their fateful singing; the slippery seal-king with his disloyal daughter; the divine horse of Achilles, which suddenly speaks with human voice, only once and never again thereafter, to forewarn his master of impending death; Bellerophon, who accomplishes the three deadly tasks and receives for reward the king's daughter with half the realm—all these possess the *Märchen* tang. But most of them are only motifs, the trappings of *Märchen* rather than *Märchen* fully formed; and they do not make an impressive list for two poems of such wide scope. The Iliad in particular is ill represented.

Yet if the pattern of *Märchen* be as distinctive as we have claimed, it should be possible to discover it even where Homer has most Hellenically hidden it from view. Paying heed to the magic pattern woven of supernatural event and superhuman accomplishment, let us look again at the Iliad's chief character, to see how much of *Märchen* raiment still clings to him.

Both of Achilles' parents are superhuman, since his mother Thetis is a mermaid from the depths of the sea and his father Peleus bears marks of a *Märchen* hero. Only one consistent folk tale is attached to him; but various familiar *Märchen* motifs cluster about him. In order to win his bride he clings fast to her while she, like the old man of the sea in the Odyssey, changes herself into lion and snake. Any son by her is predestined to become mightier than his sire, for which reason the high god Zeus has wisely abandoned his interest in her. The wedding feast is an affair for all the immortals, who attend bringing their gifts to the mortal groom. Peleus is the wielder of a wonderful weapon, the ashen spear which Achilles is to inherit; and a story is also told of a marvelous hunting knife which he possesses, which is stolen from him and recovered in the nick of time to save his life. At the court of Akastos he performs the *Märchen* exploit of secretly cutting out the tongues of the wild animals which he has slain, in order to produce them at the appropriate moment to refute his slanderous accusers. So liberal a share of folk tale presumably removes him from the semihistoricity of saga into the timeless and placeless world of *Märchen*. Precisely because they do not belong in the jealously prized genealogies of saga memory, *Märchen* heroes tend to stand out as lonely wanderers, as folk from far away or from nowhere. Except for his loose connection with Aiakos and through him with Aegina, where he certainly does not belong, Peleus has only an arbitrary contact with the heroic world. If he takes part in the Calydonian boar hunt and in the voyage of the Argo, these were catch-all adventures to which any unattached hero might be joined. We are not even sure just where he is supposed to have lived, since his home is Phthia yet his son Achilles comes from the Spercheios valley. No modern archaeologist has tried to dig up the palace or city of father or son.

Achilles is an equally isolated figure. Even in the crowded company of the Trojan War he lurks lonely and apart. He is not apparently an Achaean and has no part in the final Achaean capture of Troy, being the only major Greek hero to be slain during the siege; and he deliberately absents himself from the conflict (who can say whether his famous "wrath" is cause or consequence of this isolation?). Like himself, his folk the Myrmidons are a lonely race, unknown to history or saga, unrelated to Argives and Danaans and Achaeans, and so out of place in legend that a mythical origin of men made out of ants was told to account for their existence. No one who has observed the pathetic Greek trust in etymological verities will doubt that the chance echo between Myrmidon and the Greek word for ant, *myrmex,* is responsible for the myth of the ant-men; but this only confirms the suspicion that nothing real was known about them. Achilles' own name is obscure, but may derive from water and rivers, so that his stock epithet of "swift-running" may belong to him by natural right. As for his father Peleus, many moderns agree with Homer in connecting his name with the mountain Pelion, thus still further confirming him as an elemental evocation. Then the swift-running river, with a mountain for father and the sea for mother, may originally have been some sort of local hero or divinity of northern Greece, elected (for some unrecapturable reason) to become the central figure of some story, and, as such, decked out with the trappings and accouterments of folk tale. Having thus attained stature, he was attached (like Siegfried to the Burgundians) to that world of great men and heroic actions which Greek oral poetry fostered—its saga world of the Achaeans.

Without entirely subscribing to such an analysis of the swift-footed, short-lived Achilles—because etymologies are always the weakest link in any proof,—we need not dismiss such speculations as outmoded survivals of nineteenth-century abuses in mythology. In the scales in which we shall ultimately have to weigh our Homeric heroes, we must grant even etymological speculations and nature myths their appropriate weight, however slight. Whatever his ultimate origin, Achilles must derive from a different realm from the severely practical Menelaos, the garrulous old politician Nestor, or for that matter almost all the other leading figures of the Achaean expeditionary force.

Thus begotten and born of *Märchen* wedlock, Achilles in his short life is surrounded with trappings of the *Märchen* world. His mother tries to make him immortal (much as Demeter strove for the king's son whom she nursed at Eleusis); but, because she holds him by the heel as she dips him in the fire, she leaves a spot where death may enter. As in the Eleusis legend, the father unwittingly foils the nearly completed magic by voicing his alarm at the sight. Thetis in anger retires to her native sea. Unable to take her mortal child with her beneath the waves, she entrusts the infant to a wizard of the forest, Cheiron the centaur, to be reared high on ancestral Pelion in the very cave where the marriage feast of Peleus and Thetis had been held. Under Cheiron's tutelage Achilles grows to man's strength and more than man's prowess. When at length he goes to the war he takes with him his father's mighty ashen spear, which none but he among the warriors can lift, and the immortal horses which the sea-god gave his father at his wedding.

We must not be led astray from the *Märchen* track because in the Iliad Achilles behaves like an ordinary mortal amid the Achaean freebooters, sacking and pillaging the mainland towns and raiding the cattle on the mountain slopes. Even amid the careful actuality of correct topography and realistic behavior there abides an aura of the unreal and superhuman about him. He must have marvelous armor, smithied by a god, in order to enter the fight against Hector. Before his mermaid mother brings it to him, when he shows himself on the ramparts behind the Greek ships, a cloud of fire blazes magically about his head. As he mounts his car with his huge spear in hand, "the horse Xanthos of glittering feet straight nodded with his head and spoke to him . . . 'In very deed we shall rescue thee now, mighty Achilles; but thy day of death is at hand.'" Soon he must contend with a magically swollen river, against whom only the elemental fire-god can prevail. Hector is slain and Patroklos avenged and shortly thereafter the Iliad closes. But we know from other sources that Achilles did not long outlive his triumph, but was slain before Troy by an arrow in his heel, the only spot where death might enter. Thereat his mother came accompanied by all the Muses and mermaids, and from his funeral pyre lifted up her child and carried him to the White Isle at the mouth of the river Danube; and thither, says another legend, Helen the Beautiful was brought to him; and the two lived happily together for ever and ever after. Black Sea mariners shunned the island, fearing to meet the wraiths of the two lovers.

But Achilles' glittering armor, like the dragon's hoard in the Nibelungensaga, became an immediate source of grief. When Ajax and Odysseus contended for it and the decision went against Ajax, the latter slew himself in frenzied rage. But the successful contestant was wise enough to avert the curse by restoring the armor to the son of its original owner. Odysseus was well aware of its baneful power: when he meets the glowering and unforgiving shade of Ajax in the netherworld in the Odyssey, he refers to the accursed weapons "which the gods set as a bane upon the Greeks."

Who can fail to be struck by the similarities between these *Märchen*-born details attaching to Achilles and those which the Norse Volsungasaga attributes to Sigurd? Let us briefly draw the parallel. The tiny Sigurd, who has lost his father and been reft from his mother, is entrusted to the wise smith Regin to rear in the depths of the forest. When he has grown ready for adventure, he breaks every sword that Regin forges until at last a more marvelous blade is welded from the fragments of his own father's weapon. Armed with this, he slays a dragon and takes its treasure hoard. (In the Nibelunge Nôt, by bathing in the dragon's blood he becomes invulnerable save for a single spot where a fallen linden leaf clung to him.) He is warned of impending danger by the chattering woodpeckers, whose language he suddenly understands. On a magic steed given to him by a god he sets out for further adventure and an early death—a destiny which he foreknows and accepts with equanimity.

It would be neither good logic nor good method to assert that, because of these resemblances, Achilles and Siegfried are one and the same. To make such an assertion would be to misunderstand the nature of oral epic and the behavior of *Märchen*. The supernatural mechanism may be the same, almost point for point, however differently the historic environment and the other human incidents may be. Yet this might indicate only that there was a common stock of traits and motifs which might be used to make more *Märchen*-like the hero of the tale. Presumably, Achilles has as little historic right to appear amid Mycenaean chiefs on the plain of Troy as Sigurd among the Burgundian kings of the Rhineland. But otherwise the two heroes agree more in their trappings and accessories than in their actions and adventures. The wonderful weapons, the divine horses with their human speech, the accursed armor, the choice between fates, the heroic strength and swiftness—such things are common and vagrant accretions, marking Achilles as a *Märchen* figure, but not sufficing to identify him with any specific *Märchen* hero.

Structurally, the Iliad's story of the wrath of Achilles does not show the characteristic plot pattern of any known folk tale. Nor is this surprising, since, as it stands, the poem is a dramatic *novella* illustrating human character and its development through situations of intense emotional stress. Generically, it is not a folk tale at all. If we search for vestiges of *Märchen* plot in its composition, we shall scarcely make any very convincing discoveries. And yet there is enough basic resemblance to folk tale to leave us wondering whether some popular story, known to the Greeks but no longer familiar to us, may not have inspired the narrative and motivated the action, even as saga tradition supplied many of the names and all of the basic setting. Such a transmutation of genre is neither unparalleled nor even unlikely. Whoever has compared the Nibelungenlied with the Volsungasaga has seen this conversion of the supernatural and physically irrational events of folk tale into a close-knit "drama of human motives, depending for its development on the interplay of human passions and activities." Quite as drastic as the careful reduction of the floating saga of Troy to the topography of a few square miles of actual terrain at the mouth of the Scamander, is the reduction of a foot-free folk tale with its rambling marvels to the unified and self-contained behavior of a wholly human situation.

Again, for Homer, Briseis and Chryseis are chattels, part of the booty of war to be distributed among the Achaeans together with the other livestock, armor, and material plunder from the captured mainland towns. Achilles' honor is slighted not because Briseis is a woman, but because Agamemnon has highhandedly seized what was not his and was Achilles'. A present-day field commander, by arbitrarily removing a distinguished service medal from his adjutant's uniform because he had mislaid his own, could start a magnificent personal feud without erotic complications. Achilles' grievance against Agamemnon is almost as unromantic. In Homer's eyes, it is Achilles and Patroklos who are romantically attached: the women, as women, hardly count. Yet one may at least make the query whether the story had always taken just this turn. Briseis the maiden (as we at first think) turns out to be a young widow with a story, and later in the poem when the dead body of Patroklos is brought in where she may utter the women's traditional lament for the dead, her grief is a little too genuine. Achilles was her captor and master: why this intensity of sorrow, touching on despair, over her master's friend? We can only wonder: Homer will tell us nothing.

The correct conclusion—I submit—is that even as historic fact and actual past event are vague and distant for the Iliad, so folk tale, too, with its characteristic plots and patterns, is in the Iliad elusive and remote. Indeed, Folk Tale may have had even less to do than Saga in the making of the poem. But with Saga and Folk Tale removed, we are left with only Fiction on which to hang our epic.

◇ ◇ ◇

Is the Iliad, then, all but sheer invention? And if so, was it a single deliberate invention, or a residue and accumulation from many epic efforts upon a common theme? Modern criticism has come to see—though not always to admit in quite such explicit terms—that these far-reaching questions must yield precedence to analytically prior ones, on which their own turn depends. The really cogent first questions to ask about the Iliad are these: "What is its structural form?" and then, in the second place, "How completely does this form inform it?"

There are entire volumes, as well as shorter essays, on the structure of the Iliad. But has the Iliad any structure? A modern reader, lost in the combat scenes and not too tensely expectant to discover who is next to kill whom, and how, may in momentary petulance make a negative reply: such bloody junketing is mere disconnected episode. But dwelling on detail for detail's sake is oral narrative's eternal prerogative, and in itself neither proves nor disproves anything. Just as we have already stripped from the central hero his Siegfried trappings because they seemed to be accessory borrowings from the glittering stage wardrobe of fairy tale, so we shall have to strip from the poem itself its trappings of paladin combat, applying the reasonable criterion that only a battle which affects the movement of the plot shall be permitted to remain. Now what is left? And has it any recognizable form?

Except for Aristotle I can recall no critic ancient or modern who has made the obvious observation that the Iliad's structural type form is that of Attic drama and that its unity consequently is to be judged by the standards of fifth-century dramatic art.

Only, where Attic drama remains true to the compactness and brevity of literature that has not been a written creation for very long, the preceding Ionian epic must be allowed the copiousness and amplitude of scale which belongs to the heyday of long-established oral composition.

Obviously, any critic will be hesitant to scrutinize Homeric epic through the lenses of fifth-century Attic drama because of the violent anachronism such a procedure implies. However, though the *physical* ancestor of Attic tragedy may have to be sought in Dionysiac mummers' choruses, or wherever else you will, its direct *spiritual* ancestor is certainly Homer. Many a page of the Iliad could be edited for Attic stage presentation with a minimum of alteration. The speeches are already there for the two or three actors, and the accompanying narrative is not more than can be converted into stage business for the speakers. When the speeches cease and Homer himself picks up the mask, more than once we are reminded that in Attic drama, too, there is a storyteller, the Messenger, who carries the action forward until the leading character again may talk. And though we have no choruses in Homer, the dramatic pause and divertive interlude for which the tragic chorus so often serves are already well established in epic.

In short, our procedure is an anachronism only if we are not to be allowed to discover the father in the child and are denied our article of faith that the Hellenic sense for form is an enduring trait, to be identified wherever and whenever Greek creative artistic forces are at work. After all, the Athenians were the most Ionic of the mainland Greeks; so that it may not be so strange if an identical sense for that logical mastery over emotional resources and that vivid actuality in the representation of human beings in speech and conduct which dominates Athenian written drama had already asserted itself generations earlier in Ionian oral epic. I can only beseech your patience in this untried attempt to find in Attic tragedy the key to the structural form of the Iliad.

If we select Sophocles' *Oedipus Rex* as a master pattern from which to derive the basic structural norm of Greek drama, there would seem to be a rather clear clue to the method of its making. Most characteristically, movement toward calamity or other denouement, though it may be relentless, is never uniform or unbroken. Its graph resembles, not a steady gradient, but a succession of peaks of tension followed abruptly by valleys of relaxation or diversion. The relaxation is accomplished by the intrusion of choral interludes during which the actors are silent, usually absent from the scene. The diversions take the form of counterplot or other means of apparent escape from the imminent outcome.

Let us apply this observation to the Iliad and consider the movement of its plot in terms of tension, interlude, and counterplot. So heavily traveled a track as the Iliad's story will perhaps seem new enough to be endurable if we tread it with eyes fixed on this structural element of dramatic form.

The prime objective of the story's action is not the capture and sack of Troy (in which the Iliad has no immediate interest), but requital to Achilles for his affronted honor. This objective is to be attained through Agamemnon's humiliation as a result of his enforced discovery that he cannot maintain his offensive against the Trojans without Achilles' assistance. Zeus has solemnly promised this issue to Thetis' supplication, so that its ultimate eventuation seems certain. Nevertheless there are various possible devices by which it might be averted. If the Greek army were to abandon the entire enterprise and return home, Achilles would be left flatly without chance of requital. Or if some peaceful agreement were reached between Trojans and Greeks, Achilles would again be robbed of his due. Or again, the issue of battle might be determined through selection of champions to represent the two opposing sides, making Achilles' intervention unnecessary. Or Paris and Menelaos, as the injuring and the injured party, might fight out the issue of Helen's abduction without further appeal to their armies.

All these devices to delay the consummation of the plot or to threaten its complete frustration are introduced into the course of the Iliad's narrative and their possibilities are explored with extreme skill. Almost at the opening of the action, Agamemnon's dream leads to a feigned embarkation order to test the Greek will to remain. The order is greeted with acclamation as the Greek army rushes headlong for the beaches. Only divine intervention prevents a debacle. Paris and Menelaos next meet in single combat to decide Helen's retention or return. Paris is on the verge of defeat when again the gods intervene; Paris is removed invisibly from the fray, and the Trojan archer Pandaros is inspired to break the truce treacherously and thus throw the armies back into conflict. Thereafter Hector as champion of Troy challenges any Greek to step out as his opponent: on the outcome of their contest shall depend the issue of the war. This counterplot too comes to nothing when nightfall interrupts the battle. Thereat Paris is induced to offer reparation to the Greeks for Helen—"Her I will not give back; but all the riches I brought with her hither from Argos I am minded to return, and to add thereto from my own belongings." The acceptance of such an offer would of course have nullified the main objective of the plot, since Achilles' claim would never have been met; but the Greeks spurn the offer and the bitter strife is resumed. Through these several delaying actions the advance of the plot has been prevented for almost the first third of the poem. It is only after the removal of all these obstacles that the central dramatic development gathers headway. Zeus now intervenes to make good his promise to Thetis and give the upper hand to the Trojans. Hard-pressed at the ships, Agamemnon is constrained to make overture to the sullen Achilles and is superbly rebuffed by that self-centered youth who cannot resist the temptation to gloat over the discomfiture of his superior officer. Here is the ἀγών, or formal debate, featured near the center of many a Euripidean play. Precisely at this moment of extreme dramatic tension, like the sudden pause and shift which choral ode brings to Attic tragedy, there comes an interlude in the Iliad with the irrelevant story of the sortie of Odysseus and Diomede under cover of night to spy on the Trojan encampment, their capture of Dolon, a counterspy from the Trojan ranks, and their murderous foray on the Thracian king Rhesos, newly arrived before Troy with horses—"the finest that ever I saw" (says Dolon), "and the largest, more shining than snow and like unto the winds to run."

With the resumption of the main story after this diversion, it would seem as if the final outcome could now no longer be postponed. But the poet devises two more counterplots. Achilles, still unwilling to put aside his wrath, sends Patroklos in his stead, arrayed in Achilles' own armor and mounted on Achilles' car, to drive the Trojans from the ships. Had Patroklos prevailed too triumphantly, the main objective would once again have been jeopardized because he, rather than Achilles, would have won the glory. Still worse—and shrewdest counterplot of all,—at the height of the battle Hera seduces Zeus on the flower-bright peak of Mount Ida and thereby robs the Trojans of their greatest helper. As a result, Hector is wounded and the Trojan cause seems destined to collapse and with it the main objective, the assuaging of Achilles' wounded pride. Now comes the final reversal of direction, the *peripeteia* without which no good Attic play can move. The counterplots are frustrated: Zeus awakes and remedies his heedlessness; Hector is revived, and slays Patroklos. Now at last the true (and truly tragic) outcome is in sight. And again, immediately after so climactic a moment of dramatic tension, the scene shifts to an emotionless interlude. As in Attic tragedy the hard sharp dialogue of the striving actors suddenly gives place to the lyric quiet of chorus with its opulent splendor of word and its actionless beauty of remote allusion, so here in the Iliad all the deadly contest and the dramatic characters are suddenly dropped from sight. We are on Olympus and the lame god of the forge is fashioning all manner of marvelous scenes on the circles of a great new shield, while Thetis waits, chatting with Charis. The second third of the great poem is ended.

As in an Attic play, the final action runs a swifter course; Achilles and Agamemnon are reconciled, and Achilles, seeking vengeance for Patroklos, goes forth to battle for the Greeks. But once again, and now for the last possible time, the devices of counterplot and interlude are both employed. The counterplot hinges on the danger that Achilles will be drowned in the raging Scamander before he can achieve his deed of prowess; and the interlude, following hard on the tensely told climactic slaying of Hector, is the leisurely account of the funeral games for Patroklos with their racing of chariots and harmless striving of heroes. As in an Attic play, the end does not come with some final horror or new crisis, but with the resolution of every still unresolved element of action and an attainment of final calm. As Achilles gives Hector's body back to King Priam, all the bitterness between Greece and Troy is transmuted into a resigned sorrow. This, and not the wild sack of Troy, is the end.

Add to such an analysis the obvious corollary observation that the opening books of the poem closely resemble in their function the prologue of a tragedy, explaining the situation and introducing the characters, and the Iliad's astonishing similarity of structure to Attic drama is manifest. Only in the long narratives of battle with their (to us, at least) monotonous and unedifying maiming and murdering of hapless men does the oral epic manner betray its loquacity and offend against the close coherence of drama.

This organic dramatic unity which the Iliad reveals is not in itself sufficient proof of the unity of its authorship, since the Argument from Design has never been acknowledged to be conclusive. Yet the close adherence to so complex a form should certainly prejudice us toward a belief in a personal divinity, a Θεῖος Ὅμηρος, as its author. But whether the compositors were one or many, the application of such an all-embracing dramatic pattern goes far to confirm the suspicion that in the Iliad there has been a profound fictional disturbance and transformation of the traditional material of Saga and Folk Tale. For Saga, unaided, maintains a much more casual sequence; and while *Märchen* too have form, theirs is a form characteristically their own and totally different from that of drama and dramatic narrative. *Märchen* delight in stringing incidents and adventures like beads on a necklace. And though *Märchen* understand dramatic situations and often make the most of them when they arise, they know little of the emotional compression and expansion which give dramatic plot its tremendous power and they have little gift for looking forward and backward in order to keep track of human motives and the complex interactions of human character. All these the dramatic artist must supply; and all these—if they really be as patently present in the Iliad as we have supposed—must be classed as fiction and credited to the epic poet's own powers of invention.

Precisely because the dramatic unity of the Iliad's plot is so fully elaborated, it is impossible to find intact the folk tales out of which it was built. Only the accessories of the *Märchen* heroes, which have as little disturbing effect on the underlying dramatic movement as costume or scenery, will survive unedited. Hence it comes that Achilles may drive deathless horses, swing a lance that none other can lift, wear divine armor and have a cloud of fire blaze about his head, struggle with flame against a magically swollen torrent, converse with his horses in human speech, and in general betray his origin as a *Märchen* hero, and yet not experience the typical string of disconnected magical vicissitudes which

Märchen deals in, but play the part of a recognizably human being in a rationalized conflict of human emotions. Just as fiction has had the upper hand over saga in topographical setting and cultural environment for the material exteriors of the Homeric epic, so fiction has prevailed over folk tale in the humanization of plot and the portrayal of human behavior.

◇ ◇ ◇

To what cultural epoch of Greek civilization does this fictional borrowing from the poet's own surroundings belong?

We have already seen that the material environment of the Homeric epic fails completely to report or describe the actualities of Mycenaean culture. On the contrary, it abounds in elements typical of the so-called Oriental period of early classical civilization, which immediately succeeded the Geometric phase in Greece. There are cauldrons and tripods, furniture with lathe-turned spindles, women's veils, brooches and stickpins, jewelry bearing animal designs, stained ivory, furnishings openly declared to be importations from Egypt and Phoenicia, temples housing cult statues, town walls and (in the Odyssey) town plans laid out with market place and sacred precincts. If there is no mention of money or coinage, papyrus to write on, cats in the houses, domestic fowl in the courtyards, the absence of these will deter us only from bringing our environmental date later than the seventh century.

Nor is it true that a great many different cultural periods are all represented in Homeric epic, as though it were a catch basin for the flotsam of the passing centuries. Methodologically, we are entitled to lay down two rather simple theorems: First, that if any considerable portion of the Homeric poems had come down by direct mouth-to-mouth repetition from preclassical times, it would have to preserve some accurate cultural information about the period which it purports to describe. As has already been emphasized, in this it signally fails. Second, that an accumulated poem should contain incidental references to all the various centuries in which its constituent portions were composed and accreted. Had the Iliad grown up piecemeal or gradually, with several generations of compositors adding and altering, the process should betray itself by a sort of cultural stratification in which the successive periods could be distinguished. On the other hand, if the Iliad's composition were essentially a single act wherein traditional material belonging to saga and folk tale and romantic legend was cast into a comprehensive form imposed by the necessities of fiction, it should display only two important cultural and chronological strata, widely separated in time and character. One of these would be the saga stratum, appropriate to a markedly remote past; the other, the fiction stratum, derivable from the poet's contemporary present. And even the saga stratum might be contaminated by fiction, if the poet deliberately turned from his own world in order to produce a greater impression of antiquity. In English literature, Sir Walter Scott would be an outstanding example of such fictional archaism. Fortunately, the Greek poets were little inclined to antiquarianism; yet the possibility remains that some part of Homer's heroic world which cannot be ascribed to his own experience may have come straight out of his imagination and not, as true saga should, down the long ladder of the years. The famous query, Why do the Homeric chieftains never eat fish? may have been correctly answered by the humorless late Greek commentator who said, Because a diet of fish lacks grandeur.

We must deal very briefly with a typical and by now famous instance of attempted disintegration of Homer according to a supposed cultural stratification in the poems.

Everyone is familiar with the sequence of stone, bronze, and iron which mark with their use the successions of human material cultures. Looking for these in the Homeric poems, many have held that bronze and iron are so inconsistently represented that a distinction must be drawn between Bronze Age and Iron Age elements, a sort of disintegration according to archaeological strata or levels. Passages which showed less use of iron and more use of bronze must be older than those which showed great familiarity with iron. All this was sheer self-deception and stands up very ill under competent professional scrutiny.

Nor was the situation improved by Andrew Lang's courageous unitarian stand, by which he believed that he had proved an early date for Homer by arguing that Greece must have passed through a transitional stage when iron was coming in but bronze had not yet gone out. Since the situation has been so consistently misunderstood or misinterpreted, we must pause long enough to note how matters really stand.

In comparison with ourselves in the modern world, classical Greece never emerged from the Bronze Age at all. In fifth-century Greece, armor was made of bronze, as were all the more durable pots and pans, ewers and wine jars; of bronze were made mirrors and mirror cases, bed frames, hinge sockets, bolts, door knobs, ship fittings, awls, pins, brooches, and so on for an extremely long and tedious list. Even the normal Greek name for a smith was "bronzer" (*chalkeus*). Bronze proved itself inadequate and was regularly replaced by iron only where a sharp cutting edge was needed, as for hewing, sawing, or slicing. Hence, sword blades, knives, ax heads, and surgical lancets were made of iron or low-grade steel in classical times; whereas in Homer there is specific mention of bronze swords and bronze axes, hatchets, and pruning hooks. It is these from which all the argument and uproar spring. But otherwise there is not the slightest difference between the uses to which bronze is put in Homer and in normal classical practice: spears and spearpoints and arrowheads; helmets, shields, and leggings; cauldrons and tripods; keys, baskets, and kitchen utensils—in being made of bronze, all these are wholly normal and prove nothing for any connection with the Mycenaean Bronze Age or any "Dark Ages" immediately subsequent. On the contrary, an extensive knowledge and utilization of iron is attested by both Iliad and Odyssey: iron is worked on the anvil and tempered by being thrust red-hot into water; there are iron axes and iron knives far more frequently than bronze ones, iron fetters, and—once—iron arrowtips; and iron, as has already been remarked, is a staple article of wealth, along with gold and bronze and cattle and slaves. The whole problem therefore reduces itself very simply to the anomaly of the bronze swords and the occasional bronze axes, which alone are anachronisms in a classical context. Are they contemporary references to the poet's own experience and environment, or are they mere epic tradition, the stock-in-trade of the oral poets when they are talking battle? In this connection we may take passing notice of the great shelter shields, so heavy and clumsy that they can barely be carried, which are introduced into battle scenes only to be overlooked and forgotten by the poet or tacitly exchanged for the portable shield of the normal armament. Like the shelter shield, the bronze swords are most readily explained as chivalresque archaisms, possibly embodying memories from much earlier times and much earlier poetry, but not in the least indicative that the passages in which they are mentioned are intact fragments of equally early poems out of which the Homeric poem has been built. Homer had to create the illusion of a remote past and of a heroic action. As others have remarked, if he made his warriors fight with bronze swords, this no more proves that he himself lived in an age of bronze swords than the fact that his heroes never eat fish proves that Homer did not know that fish were edible.

It is only if all such criteria uniformly conspire to a coherent result that we are entitled to believe in anything more than a superficial effort at evoking a heroic culture by archaistic and chivalresque touches. Scholars have discovered a veritable plethora of critical tests for disintegrating Homeric poems: they may be split up according to their knowledge of iron, according to the types of armor, according to the Aeolicisms and Ionicisms of the language, according to the metric value of an invisible digamma (which last, though it sounds ridiculous, ought to be one of the most trustworthy of all), and so on through all manner of devices archaeological, philological, and cultural. In every case the resulting pattern of the parts is a different one. No two methods, not even any two exponents of the same method, ever agree. Since only one out of all this multitude can be right, I do not think it hasty or ill-advised to suppose that all are wrong.

There are only two well-marked strata in the content of the Homeric poems: one is the stratum of saga, referable to the Mycenaean Age, based on highly remote hearsay (somewhat patched and refurbished by antiquarian imagination); the other is the stratum of fiction, referable to the poet's own age and environment.

CHAPTER V

THE SETTING OF THE ODYSSEY

TOWARD THE CLOSE of the twelfth century before Christ, not merely Mycenaean Greece and the Aegean, but all the Nearer East, sank into lethargy or fell apart. In central Anatolia the Hittite empire vanished utterly, while to the south the hitherto great and victorious Egypt grew enfeebled and aloof. Except for such brief and inconsequential invasions as that of Sheshonk into the Holy Land, Egyptian armies no longer crossed the Suez line into Palestine and Syria. On east and west the desert shut in a decadent and unambitious land; to the north lay the great barrier of the sea, whereon no Egyptian merchant vessels plied. Except for the few remnants of sea-borne Phoenician travel, hardly a foreigner now set foot on the Nile banks—least of all, Greeks from the Aegean, who were passing through a long period of depression even more severe than that which held Egypt down.

The recovery from these centuries of inertia, under the mysterious resurgence of vital energy from which civilizations are begotten, did not originate with Egypt, but reached that land from elsewhere. While Egypt still slumbered under incompetent priestly rule, split and divided, Assyria entered a phase of new brilliance which, after the middle of the eighth century, and under the Sargonid dynasty, exerted a stimulating influence through all the Mediterranean East. In Asia Minor, where the Hittite empire had long lain in ruins, Phrygia had become a rich kingdom; and on the shores of Lake Van there now flourished an Armenian dynasty whose high culture was distinguished by its skill in metallurgy. Syria, Phoenicia, Palestine, Egypt, Cyprus, and at length the isolated and commercially unprosperous Geometric culture of the Aegean islands and shores, were all affected. Indeed, so profound was the change produced by this "Oriental" contact toward the close of the eighth century, that it is not too much to say that here, if anywhere, our modern world had its birth. Alphabetic writing was adapted from Phoenician precept; written gradually displaced oral literature; commerce, industry, manufacture awoke; and with the new stirring of material prosperity the culture of classical Greece took on form and substance.

It was during this century of resurgence between the mid-eighth and the mid-seventh centuries that the Sidonians (as they called themselves and as Homer often calls them, although he also agrees with us and the later Greeks in giving them the more generic name of Phoenicians) became more frequent visitors to the Aegean, where they practiced reputable barter not unmixed with theft and petty piracy. The picture of them which the Odyssey presents fits perfectly our archaeological concept of their activities in Greek waters throughout the seventh century. During the sixth century they were ever more and more displaced in Greek markets by native Greek competitors, and before the century was even half run they had disappeared from Grecian soil.

It cannot be too strongly emphasized that in the opening phases of this stirring epoch of new awakening in Greece there is no Egyptian component. Whatever in the decorative motifs and new artistic impulses of late eighth- and early seventh-century Greek art may at first glance look Egyptian is actually so only at second hand through Phoenico-Syrian or Assyrian derivative forms. This can only mean that Egypt at this time was still inaccessible and unknown to the Greeks; for, had the Nile valley been open to Greek commerce and exploration during the eighth century, it must have formed a potent rival to the Assyrian and Syrian influences which at that time so effectively penetrated Greek art and material culture.

Beyond question, Greek classical civilization was to owe a debt to Egypt; but the period of emulation and absorption of Nilotic accomplishments began a whole century later. The inspiration to carve huge naked men of stone, standing with the left foot slightly advanced and hands clenched at their sides, came to Greece from Egypt; but the Greek "Apollos" and colossi do not begin until the reign of Psammetichos in the latter half of the seventh century. The sacred road leading up from the sea to Apollo's oracular temple at Didyma outside Ionian Miletus was lined with statues of seated priests and couchant animals in imitation of the statue-bordered approaches leading to the Egyptian temples from the landing stages on the Nile. Since the Milesians were the first Greeks to set up a trading post in the Delta (their "Milesian Fort" being an earlier settlement than Naukratis), it would be natural to conclude that they were the first Greeks to introduce the Egyptian sculptural tradition. But none of the statues of the Branchidae along the sacred road to Didyma is demonstrably earlier than the sixth century. The same sort of evidence abounds in the pottery and statuettes, the ivories and amulets and scarabs: Greece was in touch with the eastern Mediterranean in the eighth century B.C., but not in direct contact with Egypt until well along in the seventh.

The earliest pharaoh whom the classical Greeks knew from their own historical tradition was Boknrenf Uah-ka-ra, whom they called Bokkhoris. His was also the first pharaoh's name to find its way on grave offerings into the tombs of Etruria—how long after his own brief reign we have no exact means of knowing. He died tragically, perhaps spectacularly by being burned alive by an Ethiopian conqueror, in 712 or 711 B.C. While the memory of him was still alive, the first Greeks reached the Delta. They found Egypt in political turmoil, so that it was debatable whether the mercenary or the merchant could find more profit. It would seem that the professional soldier opened up the land ahead of the peaceful trader.

Herodotos recounts that "the Greeks adopted three inventions from the Carians. It was these who first put crests on their helmets, devices on their shields, and armbands to carry them. Until then, shields had been controlled by leather straps worn around the neck and across the left shoulder." This statement obviously refers to the shift, which the Iliad also reflects, from the practice of fighting with only the protection of a large shelter shield to the use of bronze body armor like that of the classical hoplite, whose body covering of helmet, corselet, and leggings made a small parrying shield sufficient defense. Thanks to this superiority of equipment, the Carians and Asia Minor Greeks had become redoubtable soldiers, ready to offer their services as professional mercenaries to the best paymaster. We first hear of them in collision with the powerful Assyrian armies in 698 B.C. on the plains of Tarsus. A little later, when Gyges set up his new Lydian kingdom on the ruins of the Phrygian empire, he took these "men of bronze" into his service; and still a little later when Psammetichos revolted against the brief Assyrian rule over Egypt, Lydian Gyges seems to have conspired to assist him with his mercenaries. Perhaps it had been discovered that the Aegean hoplites were an answer to Assyrian invincibility. In any event, we know from Herodotos and from official chronicle that Ionian and Carian soldiers served under Psammetichos against the Assyrians in the middle of the seventh century. Then was founded the last great native dynasty of Egypt, which threw the Delta open to the Greeks. Mercenary service with the pharaoh persisted among the Ionian Greeks for a hundred years longer. Far up the Nile at Abu Simbel, on the legs of one of the colossi of a temple façade, one still may read the carved names of Greek participants in the Nubian expedition of 589 B.C. By then, the days of armed pilfering had long been over, and Greek commerce was firmly established in the land. Under the next ruler, Amasis, the most philhellene of the dynasty, Naukratis near the westernmost arm of the Nile became a truly Greek town, the first in Egypt.

Thus, if we combine the Greek account with modern archaeological evidence, we shall believe that there were no Greeks in Egypt during the eighth century, that armed freebooters raided the Delta in the first half of the seventh century, that with the restoration of stable government under Psammetichos at the middle of the century these freebooters became mercenaries in the king's service, and that during the closing decades of the century mercantile profit overweighed military gages, leading to the peaceful commercial relations which made Egypt so familiar to the Greeks during the sixth century.

The first entrance of Greek mercenaries into the pharaoh's service is recounted by Herodotos in a famous passage wherein he tells how Psammetichos of the Saïte nome

> sent to the city of Buto where was the most reliable of the Egyptian oracles. Thence there came to him a prophecy that he should be avenged when men of bronze appeared from the sea. Now, great unbelief was shed upon him that brazen men should come to his succor; and yet no great time elapsed before certain Ionians and Carians bent on piracy were forced to land on Egyptian soil. And when these had so come, all armored in bronze, an Egyptian who had never before seen men so accoutred came to Psammetichos in the marshes with the report that men of bronze had arrived from the sea and were plundering the plain. Thereat he knew that the oracle was being fulfilled and made friendly advances to the Ionians and Carians and with promises of great reward persuaded them into his service.

No one can read this passage in Herodotos without being reminded of an extraordinarily similar one in the Odyssey. For no apparently more cogent reason than that Odysseus dislikes to tell the truth when a lie will serve equally well, that much-traveled adventurer tells the swineherd Eumaios a yarn to cover his true identity. He pretends that he is a swashbuckling Cretan who survived the Trojan War and organized an expedition of nine ships to Egypt. There he arrived safely and "stayed his ships in the broad-flowing river." His crews, disobeying orders, began plundering, carrying off the women and children and killing the men.

The alarm quickly reached the city of the Egyptian king, with dire results for the invading Greeks. Native soldiery filled the plain, slaying many and taking others captive for forced labor.

But Zeus himself [says Odysseus] put a thought in my mind. . . . Instantly I put from my head my well-fashioned helmet, and my shield from my shoulders; my spear I cast from my hand. I went before the king's horses; I caught and kissed the king's knees. In pity he succored me; on his chariot he set me; homeward he drove me tearful. Then many threw at me their javelins, rushing to kill me, since they were mightily enraged. But he protected me. . . . And so I abode there for seven years and greatly gathered wealth amid the men of Egypt, where all gave generously.

Odysseus' imaginary Cretan obviously was taken into the military service of the pharaoh, who most strikingly resembles Herodotos' Psammetichos. Indeed, the whole incident is so perfect a parallel to the Herodotean account of the brazen men from the sea that both narratives seem modeled on the same incident. The coincidence is rather too exact for comfort, since it arouses a suspicion that either Herodotos or some informant of his was borrowing from his conscious or unconscious memories of Homer. Herodotos would scarcely have done so, deliberately; but even with him we are still too near the traditions of oral literature, with its utter lack of chronological conscience, to prevent a piece of Homeric fiction from reappearing as an item of historical record.

Fortunately, nothing hangs upon this immediate issue. Even if we should not altogether believe the historian Diodoros when he asserts that Psammetichos was the first pharaoh to abstain from killing or enslaving every foreigner who landed on Egyptian shores, we have no reason to question that he was indeed the first in many centuries to employ foreign mercenaries. As though dated, stamped, and sealed, Odysseus' invention bears on it the mark of the years just after the middle of the seventh century, after Psammetichos had taken the Carian and Ionian mercenaries into his service and before his rule was so secure that foreign plundering of the Delta had perforce given place to peaceful trading.

Another Odyssean passage exactly confirms this chronology. But to understand it we must add a geographical note to our brief historical account of Greco-Egyptian relations. The many-branched Nile—as the epithet implies—reaches the sea through several distinct channels. As they exist today, the Rosetta (anciently called the Bolbitinic) stream is the largest of the western arms, while the Canopic branch (which used to empty into the lagoons east of Alexandria) carries comparatively little water.* It was on the former stream, at the modern Sa el-Hagar, that Psammetichos made Saïs his capital city. Near its mouth (according to Strabo, whose account of the Delta is excellent) the Milesians arriving in thirty ships built a strongpoint, the first Greek trading post in Egypt, obviously placing it there because of the king's residence at Saïs. These earliest Greek visitors knew nothing of the more western Canopic branch, whose access to the sea was hidden by the lakes and lagoons through which it passed, whereas the Bolbitinic Nile was certain of discovery because it issued through a low headland directly into the open Mediterranean. The headland (below modern Rosetta) was further marked by some sort of beacon, which the Greeks called the "Watchtower of Perseus." Strabo specifically sets this landmark near the Bolbitinic mouth. Now, Herodotos takes issue with what he calls the "Ionian" definition of Egypt as consisting only of the Delta, "by which they mean the coast between the so-called Watchtower of Perseus† and the Pelusiac Brine-pits" (over near modern Port Said). If the Watchtower of Perseus was held to

* If we are to believe Herodotos' account, the situation was precisely the reverse in antiquity. The Bolbitinic Nile was for him an artificial waterway, while the Canopic was the chief western arm. I am inclined to believe that he was misinformed and that he minimized the Bolbitinic Nile, whose mouth he probably had not seen.

† Commentators are inclined to discover disagreement between Herodotos and Strabo in the location of this landmark. But a check on the reported distances (even though

bound the Delta on the west and if this beacon actually marked the mouth of the Rosetta arm, is not this proof that originally the Ionians were unaware that there was a still more western branch of the river? But this is precisely the situation in the Odyssey. There too we shall find that the Rosetta branch is known and used, while the Canopic Nile appears to be unknown. This condition was not of long duration. Saïs, the capital city, was closed to Greek navigators, whose commercial center of activity became fixed at Naukratis on the Canopic branch of the river. According to Herodotos, there was even a time when Greek commerce was entirely confined to Naukratis and Greek trading vessels were forbidden to use any other branch than the Canopic. The site of Naukratis has been excavated and the finds seem to indicate* with demonstrable precision that the Greek occupation of the site must be dated later than 625 B.C. and perhaps as late as 600 B.C.

To summarize: after Psammetichos attained power and set up his residence in Saïs in the middle of the seventh century, Greek ships (mainly Ionian) used the Bolbitinic (Rosetta) mouth of the Nile when they visited Egypt; after 625 B.C. or a little later, the Canopic mouth became known and used, and Greek trade shifted to Naukratis; during the sixth century the Canopic entirely replaced the Bolbitinic Nile, Greek commerce was confined to Naukratis, and the Bolbitinic Nile leading to Saïs was officially closed to foreign ships.

Though these details are not very complicated, they have been consistently overlooked by the Homeric commentator. They must be kept clearly in mind by the reader of the Odyssey who wishes to discover with what beautiful precision they set a date to a certain well-known passage in the poem.

---

measured in the variable unit of the *schoinos*) will show that Herodotos is quoting an early Ionic source for which the Watchtower marks the westernmost extent of the Delta because (for it) the Bolbitinic is still the westernmost branch of the river.

* The material evidence has been carefully and competently resurveyed by Gjerstad in (Liverpool) *Annals of Art and Archaeology,* XXI (1934), 67–84. He is very hesitant in admitting that the Greek occupation of the site could be earlier than 600 B.C.

In Mycenaean times a trade route from the Aegean to the Nile may have led around the eastern shore of the Mediterranean past Cyprus, Phoenicia, and Palestine; but this is not the road to Egypt in the Odyssey, where the voyage starts from Crete southward across the broad expanse of open water to the North African shore. Whether known or not to the Mycenaeans, this direct crossing to Africa does not seem to have been used by the classical Greeks until sometime near the middle of the seventh century, when its exploitation led to the colonization of Cyrene. Nestor (who had never made the trip) regards it as a venturesome journey over a waste so wide that not even the birds could cross it in a year; yet this must be traditional poetic commonplace or deliberate exaggeration, because in another passage of the Odyssey the sailing distance is given quite accurately as four days from Crete to the Nile mouth down a strong north wind. Actually, the difficulty was not so much in reaching the Nile as in getting home again, because the only sure winds during the summer sailing season were northerly and westerly, and ancient ships could not beat against the wind. This was the predicament in which Menelaos found himself when he started home from Egypt after seven years' profitable stay. He lay without sailing wind for twenty days on the tiny rocky island opposite which the great city of Alexandria was one day to rise:

> There is an island in the surging sea in front of Egypt—they call it Pharos—as far away as daylong a hollow ship might fare with shrill breeze astern. Good mooring harborage it has, whence trim ships put out to open sea after they have taken dark water aboard.

Many a commentator has impugned this passage and accused its author of ignorance and error because the isle of Pharos (which later was to hold the lighthouse for Alexandria, ancestor to all the "*phares*" of modern times) lay less than a mile offshore—which certainly is not a day's sail! But if we recall that the earliest Greek ships were coming to Egypt from the west along the

Libyan coast and that, like the Milesians who founded their trading post in the Delta, they were headed for the XXVIth-dynasty capital of Saïs on the Bolbitinic Nile, and if we further note that the name "Nile" (though classical and already used by Herodotos) does not occur in Homer, for whom "Egypt" is primarily the name of the river and only secondarily the name of the coun-

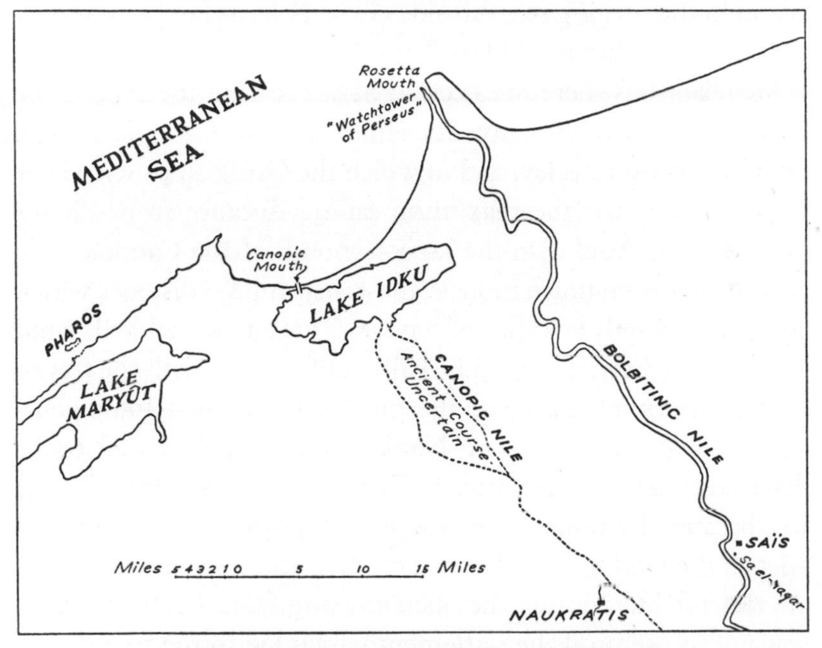

PART OF EGYPT AS RELATED TO THE ODYSSEY

try—then the verdict will prove very different and entirely favorable to Homer's accuracy. For the coasting distance from Pharos to the Bolbitinic mouth below Rosetta is more than forty miles; and since the Homeric ship probably never covered more than a hundred miles in twenty-four hours, this would involve a ten or eleven hours' sail, or, as the Odyssey phrases it, "daylong with favoring wind." Greek mariners very generally sought offshore islands for their bivouacs, since the mainland might not be safe, and Pharos was not only an island but the one protected harbor along the whole Libyan shore. It was therefore a landmark and a way station on the voyage from Greece, such as every Greek mariner would know; and the information that it lay a full daytime's sailing from the river mouth which led to Saïs would be common property among Ionian seamen. Turned into epic verse, it would yield precisely the lines of the Odyssey: "There is an island in the surging sea, this side of the Nile, as far away as daylong a hollow ship might fare."

Menelaos has therefore been at Saïs. For him the Nile is the Bolbitinic branch. He cannot be alluding to the Canopic branch, on which Naukratis lay, and to which the Greek ships were later restricted, because the maximum sailing distance from Pharos around Cape Abukir to the lagoon mouth of the Canopic Nile cannot have been much more than twenty miles, a distance which could not possibly be called a "daylong" voyage with "shrill wind astern." The Odyssey unequivocally confronts us with the transitory condition obtaining at the time of the earliest Ionic penetration of the Delta before Naukratis was opened and traffic diverted to the Canopic branch. The date must be later than 650 B.C. because Psammetichos was not in power at Saïs nor had opened the land to foreigners until then, and also because (if we are to trust Herodotos) the open crossing from Crete to Africa was not in use until the settlement which led to the foundation of Cyrene in 630 B.C. Yet the date must be earlier than the close of the century because Homer ignores the Canopic Nile and the waterway to Naukratis. Since the required conditions are fulfilled only during the period from very close to 640 to 600 B.C. at the latest, the date of the passage must lie within these limits. In its upper range this dating overlaps that which we derived from Odysseus' yarn to the swineherd. A dating between 640 and *ca.* 620 will satisfy both.

Let us take another example of chronological "bracketing" from quite a different portion of the poem.

In the nineteenth book Penelope is explaining to a beggarly stranger (who is really her own husband Odysseus) why it is that dreams do not always come true:

Twain are the gates [she says] of unsubstantial dreams; one out of horn is fashioned, the other out of ivory. Now, those dreams that come through sawn ivory deceive us, and the word they bring is unaccomplished; whereas those which issue through polished horn bring true things to pass, when a mortal beholds them.

If to the gates of ivory (*elephas*) are assigned the dreams that deceive (*elephairontai*), this is of course due to the etymological verity which we moderns would deride as a pun. Yet the opposition of horn to ivory is none the less significant for the date of the passage. Professor Wace has taught us that the source of ivory in early Greece was the interior of Syria. When contact with the Orient was established in the eighth century, disks and plaques of sawn elephant tusk began to reach Greece. Obviously these were highly prized. But late in the seventh century the supply was interrupted. The great Scythian raid of 626 B.C. threw a curtain across from Armenia to Suez, and the fall of Nineveh in 612 B.C. completed the disruption of eastern commerce. In the Aegean world *ersatz* ivory had thenceforth to be made out of horn or bone. In the sixth-century levels of the Orthia sanctuary in Sparta only bone, not ivory, is found in any quantity. It follows that the two dream gates of the Odyssey (because the notion could not antedate the Syrian ivory trade of the late eighth century, and the pointed antithesis between the two materials should stem from the late seventh century when good honest native horn or bone was perforce replacing expensive Oriental ivory) again give us a chronological clue, a little more vague than the preceding, but best interpreted in terms of the last quarter of the seventh century. Combining it with the preceding, we should have to settle on 625–620 B.C. as the optimum maximum. But naturally the exact date cannot be pressed quite so closely.

There is much else that points to a late seventh-century date for the Odyssey and nothing that I can see to force us to postulate any other period. But the most illuminating chronological hint, next to the Egyptian passages already discussed, is to be found in the general geographical outlook of the poem. There can be no doubt that southern Italy is already familiar territory. In Book 1 there is trade in metals with the south-Italian* mines; in Book 24 there is mention of a Sicilian slave woman; in Book 20 the Sicilians are in maritime connection with Ithaca. To the east, Cyprus and Phoenicia are mentioned several times; and once there is coupled with them a reference to the North African shore and Libyan sheep, a reasonable proof that Cyrene has already been colonized. But beyond these familiar lands all is marvelous and unknown; and this *mare ignotum* coincides with the area of Punic and Etruscan supremacy during the seventh and sixth centuries. Highly significant is the manner in which Odysseus with his ships is blown out of the known into the unknown world. All goes well on the return from Troy as far as the southern cape of Laconia, when a northeast wind carries the fleet wide of Cythera into the Libyan Sea. When the storm subsides, the wind-blown wanderers come ashore in the land of the Lotos-eaters. Precisely this accident befell a Samian sea captain in historical times, according to Herodotos. About 640 B.C., Kolaios was heading for Egypt by the Cretan crossing. Off the African coast his ship was caught by an easterly gale and somehow "by divine dispensation" ended up beyond the Tunisian and the Gibraltar straits in Andalusian Spain. We may think what we like about the part which tempest and accident played in this voyage of discovery along the Punic trade route; but the beginning of the Ionian exploration of the far Mediterranean West is dated by the exploit.

* I agree with those who hold that Mentes in sailing "to Temesa in quest of copper" was headed for Bruttium and not for Tamassos in Cyprus, because that town lay *inland* near the very center of the island and seems to have been inhabited by Greeks, not "men of alien speech."

West of Cyrene the North African shore turns abruptly south around a headland at which the Mediterranean winds and currents divide. A sailing vessel bearing down on this coast, if it made land east of this headland, would find itself borne eastward toward Egypt by the prevailing winds aided by a mile-an-hour current; whereas if it chanced to arrive west of the same headland, wind and current would conspire to take it toward an exactly opposite destination, south into the Gulf of Sidra and so around to the west with Tripoli and ultimately Tunis ahead. It was this latter route on which the storm drove the Samian ship in Herodotos and the fleet of Odysseus in Homer.

Down in the Gulf of Sidra the shore is marsh, sand, and rock without human habitation or even vegetation showing for several hundred miles. Then at last the desolate swamps and salt lagoons give way to a fertile fringe of littoral, with groves of date palms growing close to the sea. And where the dates grow, there is usually water to be had.

So we came to the land of the Lotos-eaters who live on a flowery food. And there we went ashore and drew water . . . and I sent out some of my men to go and discover what manner of people might be eating the food of that land. . . . And the Lotos-eaters devised not destruction for our company but gave my men the lotos to taste. And whoso ate the honey-sweet fruit cared not to come back with word, but wished to abide there with the Lotos-eaters, nibbling lotos and forgetting the journey home.

One has but to recall Hesiod's dour lament on the hard peasant toil of Greece to realize how sweet the lazy life in the date groves of Tripoli must have seemed to the first Ionian mariners who coasted this otherwise forbidding (and perhaps forbidden) shore.

If one continues west along this Tripoli coast, he will find that the scant rainfall increases and that even in summer he may run into fog and find himself suddenly stranded on a sandy beach of the jutting island of Jerba. Here is one of the most unexpectedly fertile spots in the Mediterranean, covered with thick plantations of olives and dates, fruit trees and vines. Across a narrow strait the African mainland runs up into high mountains where, since before the dawn of history, have dwelt primitive troglodytes, landsmen who were once migrants from the desiccating Sahara.

> Thither we sailed with some god for guide in the darkness, for it was night with nothing showing and a dense mist was around the ships and no moon showed in the cloudy heaven. No one beheld the island nor even saw the long waves rolling in on the beach till the decked ships ran aground.
>
> A lovely isle it is, able to bear all crops, with lush meadows by the grey sea's strand, deep soil and fertile ploughland . . . a wooded island, with wild goats numberless.

Opposite to it, "neither near nor far," lay the mountains on whose ridges dwelt the lawless Cyclopes in hollow caves, recking not of one another, but each ruling his own wife and children.

At its corners Jerba almost touches the mainland of South Tunisia; but the cave dwellers, being a Saharan race, were not boat builders and could not reach the island. So the island was uninhabited and overrun with wild animals—

> wild goats beyond counting; for no footfall of men frightens them nor do hunters come there . . . unsown and untilled lies the land, empty of men, because the Cyclopes have no red-cheeked ships nor are there shipwrights to build them boats.

As usual preferring an island for safety's sake, the Greeks who coasted this shore would have camped on Jerba and thence explored the mainland. So in the Odyssey the expedition spent a day on the island, hunting and feasting, before an exploring party put out for the opposite mainland. The evil adventure in the Cyclops' cave followed.

The Ionians do not seem to have known this African coast before the Samian voyage to Spain, when the ship was blown westward past Cyrene. But the Ionian world was small—a community of only a dozen towns with their surrounding lands—and soon every Ionian must have heard the tale. By 630 B.C. it must have been common property and ripe for epic use.

By borrowing from the actual world at a time when the stir of high adventure was in the air, the poet of the Odyssey could give even to fairy tale its setting of plausible reality. Perhaps that would have been an impossible task during certain more prosaic epochs of Greek history, but not in the seventh century when the Ionian ships were finding passage to the silverland of Spain. The Samian captain had found that passage by skirting the North African shore and braving the Punic strait. And along this same route Odysseus was made to follow till he reached the isle of the king of the winds, of which the prototype in the mariners' actual world may be Pantelleria with its sheer lava cliffs and high volcanic peak set as a floating landmark in the windy passage between Tunis and Sicily.

At this point the Odyssey abandons the direct road to Spain, even as the Ionians themselves abandoned it after the Samian ship had made its first adventurous trip. Possibly because the Punic power based at Carthage was persistently hostile, possibly because the Algerian and Moroccan shore itself was too unsafe, the sailors of Ionian Phocaea who took up the Spanish trade substituted a wholly different course. Their route led through Greek waters as far as Sardinia. Thence, avoiding the hostile Etruscans who could shut the passage by Elba between Corsica and Italy, they steered through the strait between Sardinia and Corsica into the open and often stormy expanse of the Sardinian Sea, past the Balearic Islands of Menorca, Majorca, and Ibiza to the Spanish coast between Valencia and Alicante, where the Gibraltar-like head of Ifach, a natural watchtower, gave its name of "Lookout" or "Sentinel" (*Hemeroskopeion*) to the strongpoint which the Phocaeans established on that picturesque way station. Thence the route to Andalusian Tartessus was a simple coasting journey along a not unfriendly shore.*

There are scholars who refuse to believe that the Ionian trading vessels ever crossed such great stretches of open sea. Some even hold the opinion that Greek mariners came ashore every nightfall for food and water and sleep, and that this—quite as much as their fear of storms—explains their insistence on hugging the land. Yet the Odyssey gives us evidence that the direct crossing to Egypt was in use, that the stars were used to sail by (a puzzling matter for those who think that the Greeks navigated only by day), and that long trips in continuous voyaging were sufficiently usual to produce the metrical commonplace of such Odyssean lines as "Six days together we sailed, by night and by day." It is out of these long crossings to Africa and Spain that there came into Ionian epic the new note of great distances and stormy open waters which is not heard in the Iliad. To an attentive ear the "surge and thunder of the Odyssey" is not the splash of Aegean foam but the deeper sound of the newly opened western seas. These are no longer the little distances of the island-studded Aegean, but the larger open waters of the latter seventh century when the narrow fifty-oared ships came into use for the far Ionian voyages which opened up the Adriatic, the Etruscan, and the Spanish seas. The Odyssey rings of the West, as it rings of exploration and buccaneering. *Ex nihilo nihil;* and even the most fantastic tale must somewhere strike root on this planet. Although I do not doubt that Mycenaean ships made long journeys, I cannot persuade myself that the intimate detail of the Odyssean descriptions could have survived so many centuries of oral transmission. And since, after the Mycenaean days, Greek ships did not again sail west through the Sicilian strait until the eighth century nor

* A most welcome archaeological confirmation that Greeks really reached Tartessus during the period set by Herodotos' account has recently been made. North of Gades in the bed of the Guadalete some twelve miles above its mouth an archaic Greek bronze "pot" helmet has come to light. Competent authorities have dated its type close to 625 B.C. (*Forschungen und Fortschritte,* XV, 1939, 44 f., A. Schulten).

reach Tunisian and Sardinian waters until the seventh, I am forced to conclude that if the stimulation of actual scenes lurks behind the Odyssean narrative, then the Ionian journeys to the West are by far the most plausible source. For me, they are the only possible source.

Six days together we sailed, by night and by day, and on the seventh we reached the steep stronghold of Lamos, far-gated Laestrygonia, where herdsman hails herdsman as he drives in his flock and the other driving out makes answer. Double wages could a man earn if he took not sleep, one wage for tending cattle, one for pasturing white sheep; for the daytime and the nighttime trails are nigh at hand.

The simple enigma [illegible] these lines has long ago been solved. To this day during the heat of summer in marshy lands where the insects drive the cattle to frenzy, the kine are shut in for the night while the heavy-fleeced sheep, which can brave the flies and mosquitoes, graze in the freshness. But during the day the sheep take refuge from the sun, while the cattle must take their turn at pasture. Such a condition was probably unfamiliar to the Greeks, but has long prevailed on the swampy and malarial coast of Sardinia, where too may still be seen curious stone fortress-houses as of a race of giants. But the "wonderful harbor" of far-gated Laestrygonia is not in Sardinia, but across the narrow strait at the southernmost tip of Corsica. What a harbor that was! Once seen, it was sure to stick in a sailor's memory and be talked about, home in Ionia.

Around it on either side was wrought continuous the towering rock; at the entrance projected jutting headlands opposite each other; and narrow was the passageway between.... Within the roadstead... no wave ever billowed, either great or small; but a shining calm lay round it.

From Pantelleria past the west head of Sicily and up the eastern shore of Sardinia it is a trifle more than four hundred miles to

Bonifacio and would have been five or six days' sail for a Homeric ship. If the Sardinian strait was rough and the winds contrary (as is often the case between the two islands), shelter was offered in the calm of a marvelous harbor, as spectacular as anything in all the lovely Mediterranean. Its outer cliffs rise two to three hundred feet sheer, and are hollowed out beneath by the waves into caverns where the rock pigeons can nest—which may give us the clue to the name "Laïs-trygōn-ia." Headlands like a great gateway enclose a narrow curving stretch of harbor which leads where no rough water penetrates. Only the west wind stirs the glassy calm, and even then, with a gale keeping all shipping stormbound, only tiny waves trouble far-gated Bonifacio. At the head of the long inlet there is a beach such as Greek mariners sought and beyond it a valley with a spring of running water, a place like Artakia at which to meet the king's daughter.

The welcome which the fleet of Odysseus received was hardly in keeping with the idyllic security of this marvelous haven:

> Loud he shouted; and they ran together from every side, not men but giants. From the cliffs they cast on us huge rocks as large as men; and instantly there arose from the ships an evil din of men dying and of boats shattering. As though spearing fish, they bore off their horrible feast.*

Odysseus escaped with a single ship from Laestrygonia and sailed . . . who knows whither? We have already seen that Circe's palace belongs in the forest of European fairy tale. The Sirens on their flowery meadow are nixies, river sprites,† whence the dead-

* In A.D. 1421 the ships of Alfonso of Aragon crowded into the deep landlocked harbor of Bonifacio and laid siege to the town on the headland. After a time the Genoese came to the rescue and in turn bottled up the Spanish ships in the harbor. There followed a terrific battle, in which the modern Laestrygons joined and, as one account phrases it (utterly unconscious of the Odyssean parallel), "ship jammed against ship in the narrow channel, with the Bonifacians hurling firebrands, harpoons, and all kinds of missiles on such of the enemy's ships as they could reach from the walls." "Harpoons"—"as though spearing fish": down through the centuries Bonifacio seems to have been a death trap for the unwary.

† Greek mythological tradition made them daugters of Acheloos, the river *κατ' ἐξοχήν*.

liness of their lure. Scylla with her "six mightily long necks" with a terrible head on each, armed with three rows of close-set deadly teeth, with her body in a cave and her arms out fishing and feeling around the reef, is unmistakably a devilfish, weirdly disguised by the incurable Greek propensity to seek for etymological verities in words, so that a beast with so puppy-like a name as Scylla must bark like a puppy (*scylax*) to the immortal confusion of the resultant picture. Charybdis is probably one of the entrances to the underworld, like the "swirling pool" that led to the "vast sea bottom" in Beowulf or ultimately (I supppose) the deep well down which the heroine falls in Grimm's *Frau Holle.* If in the Odyssey the whirlpool under the fig tree, which exposes the black sand of the sea bottom when it gulps back its flood, swells and subsides three times in every day, we can only agree with Strabo that the poet had heard tell of the refluent Atlantic tide and conclude again that he had been talking with his Ionian kinsmen who had visited Andalusia beyond Gibraltar.

But all these later adventures are unlocalized; and the imaginary character of their setting betrays itself by internal contradictions. The rudest sketch which takes account of the direction of the winds in the Homeric text will demonstrate that the trip from Circe's isle past Scylla to the Island of the Sun-god cannot be reconciled with the return through the strait of Charybdis. When Odysseus visits the underworld, he sails a day's journey south from Circe's isle, lands in the eternal fog of the land of the Cimmerians (or Kemmerians or Kerberians—the confused manuscript tradition suggests that the actual historic name Cimmerian is not the original one), and ascends the river Okeanos (which for Homer bears no resemblance to the Atlantic Ocean). None of this is Mediterranean geography, but only a vague wandering through unknown water expanses somewhere out beyond Sardinia in the unexplored. The late seventh-century Greeks had no idea what lay between Spain and Africa.

The strait which held Scylla and Charybdis was only a bowshot wide and on one side of it rose a peaked mountain with an unyielding black cloud upon it (Homer has heard of the volcanoes, whether Vesuvius or Stromboli or Etna) running up as smooth as though it were polished, "so that no man may climb it, had he twenty hands and feet." So the *"Glasberg"* of European fairy tale somehow fuses with the Italian volcano to mark the way to the Thrinacian island where the Sun-god keeps his sacred kine, a domain probably as indefinite in Homer's imagination as the place where the Sun himself sets in the western flood. So in the latter part of Odysseus' adventure fiction yields to folk tale, and the late seventh century to the timeless world of faërie. Even in the earlier episodes, though there were gigantic stone houses for Greeks to see in Sardinia, and sheer lava cliffs like metal walls on the southwest approaches to Pantelleria, and primitive cave dwellers in southern Tunisia, and oasis folk living indolently off their date palms in Tripoli, yet these too are blent with elements of folk tale and fairy tale, betrayed by their supernatural size or accomplishments. Thus "Rock-pigeon-land" with its conspicuous "far-gated" entrance seems set at Bonifacio in the Sardinian strait; but it is inhabited by giant ogres who spear their victims like fish and eat them. On Pantelleria houses the king of the storm who can put all the winds in his sack and has married his six daughters to his six sons. Opposite the fertile island of Jerba with its wild goats untroubled by hunters lives a one-eyed giant so huge that he can seal his cavern with a rock such as twenty-two four-wheeled wagons could not drag from its threshold; he dashes out the brains of puny mortals like puppies' with a single blow against the ground and eats two men for supper and another two for breakfast. Even the flowery lotus exerts a spell such as belongs to the food and flowers of enchantment.

Just as in the Iliad it was saga which was deftly localized in the world of everyday beside the Ionian trade route to the Sea of

Marmora, so in the Odyssey it is folk tale (that properly has no dwelling place) which has been set down in the actual Mediterranean. Being full of marvels, it has been pushed to the least familiar corners of the Inland Sea, though still with enough of actuality in its descriptions to let us guess where the Ionian mariners have been sailing to provide such backgrounds for their Ionian poet.

The argument is easily summarized. It maintains that the fictional setting of borrowed reality behind the fairy-tale adventures which Odysseus gravely recounts to his Phaiakian hosts is drawn from the African coast of Tripoli and Tunis, from Sardinia, and more vaguely from the journey to Andalusian Spain. But these were the waters and the shores which were guarded by Carthage and Etruria and which the Greeks did not penetrate until the great resurgence of Ionian exploration swept all barriers aside and brought the Greek traders past Gades to Tartessus on the Atlantic. The fact of that Ionian penetration of the West is established for us by Herodotos. Its date is also known to us: it was the third quarter of the seventh century.

Always the same critical date emerges, with the various passages with their overlapping chronology confining its limits still more closely to the decade around 630–620 B.C. And since no other date anywhere transpires, and so much of the fabric of the poem is involved in this late seventh-century cultural environment, is it too much to conclude that this was indeed the period of its composition?*

* The references to well-established commercial relations with Egypt and to Greek mercenary service in New Babylon protract the activity of the Lesbian lyric poets Sappho and Alcaeus into the sixth century. But there is no reason for challenging Archilochos' place in the middle of the seventh century. Oral epic as exemplified by the Odyssey must therefore have overlapped the opening phases of iambic and elegiac written literature in Greece. There is not the slightest objection to such a presumption of contemporary existence of the two alien literary forms.

CHAPTER VI

THE CULT OF THE SLEEPING BEAR

In the vast storehouse of Frazer's *Golden Bough* is the following account of a bear ceremony from far northeast Asia:

The Aino of Saghalien rear bear cubs and kill them with . . . ceremonies. We are told that they do not look upon the bear as a god but only as a messenger whom they despatch with various commissions to the god of the forest. . . . An orator makes a long speech to the beast, reminding him how they have taken care of him. . . . "Now," he proceeds, "we are holding a great festival in your honor. Be not afraid. We will not hurt you. We will only kill you and send you to the god of the forest, who loves you. . . . You will ask God to send us, for the winter, plenty of otters and sables, and for the summer, seals and fish in abundance. Do not forget our messages." . . . To this discourse the bear, more and more surly and agitated, listens without conviction; round and round the tree he paces and howls lamentably till, just as the first beams of the rising sun light up the scene, an archer speeds an arrow to his heart.

It is deemed important that the bear should die instantly, without outcry and without struggling. There is no hatred for the victim, which has often been a village pet and reared by the women from a small cub. On the contrary, they feast him and make much of him, for he is their honored emissary. They do not believe that he dies truly, but that his soul will return and become a bear again in his old haunts after it has secured for them the fulfillment of their wishes from the Great Spirit, who is the lord of the mountain.

In classical times, in the northern part of the present kingdom (or whatever it may be) of Bulgaria, there dwelt a Thracian people called Getai, whom Herodotos found noteworthy because of their practice of a peculiar ritual connected with their belief in immortality:

They consider [he writes] that they themselves do not die, but that whoever perishes goes to the spirit SALMOXIS, the same whom some of them name BELEIZIS. Every four years they choose one of their number by lot and, after instructing him in their various wishes and needs, send him away as a messenger to Salmoxis. And this is how they send him. While some of them group themselves, holding three javelins, others seize the feet and hands of him who is to be despatched to Salmoxis and swinging him up into the air let him fall on the spear-points. If he is transfixed and dies, they deem the god is auspicious; but if he does not die, they put the blame on the messenger, declaring that he is a sinful man, and after they have thus found him at fault, they send off another as messenger. It is before he dies that they communicate to him their wishes.

In this Getan practice the tribesman has taken the place of the tribal animal as emissary: a man, not a bear, is sent. That is because the bear has here become the divinity, the great spirit to whom the message is sent and with whom the dying Getai may expect to live forever.

It is no new theory among students of religion that Salmoxis was a bear. We have only to listen to the rest of Herodotos' account to perceive that this identification must be correct. After remarking that these same Thracians who send away the messenger to Salmoxis "shoot arrows at the thunder and lightning, defying the god [to wit, of course, the *Greek* god, Zeus of the thunderbolt], since they believe in no other god than their own," Herodotos proceeds to relate the following remarkable anecdote:

As I learn on inquiry from the Greeks on the Hellespont and the Black Sea, this Salmoxis was a man who had been a slave at Samos for none other than Pythagoras. After gaining his freedom he amassed considerable wealth and returned with it to his native land . . . and there he built a banqueting hall in which he entertained the leading citizens and in the course of the feasting set forth his doctrine that neither himself nor his guests nor yet their children's children should die, but should come to that very place and there should live forever in enjoyment of every happiness. But all the while that he was saying this, he was engaged in making for himself an underground chamber; and when it was completed, he disappeared from among the Thracians by descending into the underground chamber, and there he abode for a space of three years. The rest lamented and mourned for him as dead. However, in the fourth year he reappeared among them; and thus they were confirmed in what Salmoxis had told them. This is the story. For my own part, as to this underground chamber and the rest, I do not precisely doubt, nor yet do I altogether believe. Still, I am of the opinion that Salmoxis must have lived long before Pythagoras. But whether Salmoxis was indeed a human being or some sort of native divinity among the Getai, let us now bid him farewell.

Whoever is familiar with the Greek propensity to rationalize the supernatural and to humanize every myth will recognize that the slave of Pythagoras (whence, of course, the poor barbarian derived his knowledge of immortality!) and the leading Thracian citizen who entertained his townsmen in a community eating hall are typical Hellenic interpretative contributions to the story. With these removed, we are left with an immortality cult centering on a mysterious exponent who feasts, then retires to an underground dwelling, pretends to be dead, is considered dead by others, but at length reëmerges to prove that death is not the end. Fortunately there are a few further ancient references to Salmoxis besides this famous Herodotean account. From these we learn that he fasted and starved himself in his self-imposed prison; that his underground chamber was a "cavelike place"; and that he took his name from the Thracian word for hide, *zalmo,* because he was dressed in a bearskin—an etymology which, by leaving the bear out of the hide, admits more than it pretends to explain!

Surely it is not very difficult to read such a riddle. The *daimon* who wears a bear's hide, who feasts heartily, then retires to fast in a secret cavelike dwelling in the ground, vanishing from mortal ken to be given up for dead, yet after a time returns to life and his old haunts, can be none other than the hibernating bear, whose mysterious, foodless, midwinter sleep has everywhere made of him a supernatural spirit to the wondering mind of primitive man.

The gruesome practice of human sacrifice, incident to the dispatch of a tribal emissary to the invisible god, seems in time to have been abolished by the Thracians, even as all such practices eventually disappeared from among other ancient races. Almost half a thousand years after Herodotos, Strabo testified to the continuance of Salmoxis worship in the Danubian area, but made no mention of human sacrifice. Instead, a gentler way of communing with the god seems to prevail:

> It is recounted that a man of the Getai, Zamolxis by name, after serving Pythagoras as a slave [so far, the source is obviously Herodotos], having learned celestial lore . . . returned to his homeland, where he was held in high esteem by rulers and people for sake of his meteorological predictions.*

The bear has become a weather prophet! But in truth he is so, nearly wherever he is worshiped; and the Salmoxis worshipers who shot their arrows at thunder and lightning were practicing weather magic. Strabo continues his account of Salmoxis (whose name he inverts to Zamolxis):

> Because of his competence in such heavenly pronouncements he at length persuaded the king to accept him as co-regent; then, after being at first merely the appointed priest of their most revered god, he came in time to be addressed as that god himself. Whereupon he took over a cavernous spot, from which everyone was excluded, and there he abode, seldom consorting with those of the outside world with the exception of the king and his attendants. This practice has endured down to our own times, there being always such an intermediary between the king and the god. The mountain [where the cave was] is held sacred and is so termed.

* ἐπισημασίας, "signs of the seasons." In popular tradition, the bear retires for the forty days following the winter solstice: his reëmergence is a sign of spring's return. Primitive societies in an agricultural state, dependent for their very life on their adaptations to the seasonal changes, might well be superstitious about meeting the first bear of the new year.

If we are to take this account literally, we shall have to conclude that among the Dacians (of whom Strabo is writing in this passage of his seventh book) the Salmoxis priest identified himself with his god and took up his abode in the sacred bear den, where he could be consulted by king and nobles as an oracle, specifically for the changing seasons. We hear nothing of the messenger dispatched to the god by slaying, and nothing of the disappearance and epiphany of the god, except as it is implied in the withdrawal of the priest-god within his cave on the sacred mountain.

Near the close of Euripides' *Rhesos* there is a curious passage in which the Muse who was mother of the slain Thracian king makes this puzzling prediction about her son:

He shall not enter earth's sombre soil: this boon shall I claim from the Bride of the underworld, Demeter's child, to release his soul, since she is bound to show honor unto the friends of Orpheus. Although unto me his mother he shall forever be as one dead that looks not on the light, since never he may come to where I am nor see me again, yet shall he live, hidden in cavern of the silver-veined earth, a spirit in human form; there shall he lie agaze, even as Bacchus' prophet dwelling within Pangaian mount, a god revered unto his votaries.

The passage has been much discussed; and certainly there is much about it that is uncertain or obscure. Yet I cannot doubt that it refers to the Salmoxis cult or that it can best be understood by glossing it with Strabo's account of the oracular cave priest of that divinity. Here, too, is a holy mountain with a cavern in which the oracular *daimon* lies concealed. The "spirit in human form" (*anthropodaimon*) hidden in a cave as though dead, like a prophet within the sacred Thracian mountain, so strongly resembles the sacred hibernating bear and the story of Salmoxis who retired to an underground chamber and was accounted dead that I cannot but believe that these supply us with the solution to the riddle.

Mount Pangaion is very close to Greek soil, being situated only a few miles north of Amphipolis. Not far from there, at Potidaea on good Greek territory, Socrates (in the pages of Plato's *Charmides*) professed to have encountered Zamolxis healers who gave him a drug and taught him a spell to cure headache. But it does not seem ever to have been remarked that the oracular and healing cult of this strange Thracian divinity penetrated much farther into Greece than this northern fringe. There was a district in central Greece, south of the Copaic basin in the hill country between Parnassos and Helikon, where Thracian immigrants or invaders must have settled in very early times. King Tereus of Daulis, of the sad Philomela story, was accounted a Thracian; the oracular seat of Abas, near by, was connected with the Thracian tribe of the Abantes; the Muses of Mount Helikon are called Thracian; and there are traditions about Thracians at Delphi and at various other spots in Phokis and northeastern Boeotia. In the heart of this old Thracian enclave, on the slope of Mount Laphystion, was situated the famous cave oracle of Trophonios.

In the reign of the Emperor Nerva, an itinerant fanatical preacher of Pythagorean doctrines, Apollonios of Tyana, visited and inspected this strange spot. His biographer, Philostratos, gives us this description of it:

> The entrance, available only to those who seek an oracle, lies in a hillside a little above the sanctuary proper. It is completely enclosed by an iron grill, and one can work one's way inside only by sitting down. Consultants are introduced, dressed in white raiment, with honey-cakes in their hands to pacify the snakes.... This is the only known oracle which gives responses through the consultant himself.

(Parenthetically, this last is a remarkable property, since Greek oracles regularly employ a "medium," whether *mantis* or *sibyl*). There appears to have been strong local objection to permitting so redoubtable an investigator of religious phenomena to inspect the mechanism of the oracle; but Apollonios succeeded in overriding the opposition and obtained permission to enter the sacred cave. He stayed underground for seven days (which was considered a record) and finally emerged clutching . . . a new edition of the teachings of Pythagoras! Philostratos adds that "the book is still preserved today in the royal villa at Antium."

In his essay *On the Daimon of Socrates* Plutarch tells of a consultant of this cave oracle who "remained two nights and a day underground; and when most people had given him up for dead and his family was mourning him, at early dawn he emerged radiant"—which evidently implies a rite of resurrection to new life after feigned or apparent death, and distinctly reminds us of Salmoxis and his promises.

But the fullest account of the Trophonian cave is to be found in Pausanias' *Descriptive Tour of Greece:*

After purification and copious preliminary feasting in a special building—a very interesting detail!—the consultant must sacrifice a ram in a pit (very much as Odysseus does when he wishes to consult the underworld prophet Teiresias), then bathe in the river, attended by two thirteen-year-old boys who have the title of Hermes, and finally drink of the cavernous sources of the river from two fountains called Forgetfulness and Remembrance, after which he is shrouded in white linen. (The underworld references are thus entirely obvious.) Next the consultant is led up to the cave in the hillside, where he beholds a cleft in the ground, artificially enlarged to a sort of hollow room six feet in diameter and about twelve in depth, whose floor he may reach by a light portable ladder. At the bottom of this he discovers a tiny hole, not seemingly large enough to crawl through; yet through it he must pass, feet first, finally slipping as though sucked or drawn into a secret inner chamber. Whatever he sees or hears in this airless place he must afterward recount to the priests, although he often emerges in such a state of terror and bewilderment that it is some time before he can laugh again.

More than one ancient source asserts that the location of the oracular cave was first revealed to men by a swarm of bees. In Suidas there is a rather haphazard remark that originally some Boeotians fleeing from advancing Thracians took refuge in the cave. But we learn more about the true nature of the place from a scholiast on Aristophanes' *Clouds* who asserts that Trophonios was actually a human being with a longing for notoriety who drew attention to himself by retiring underground. A yet more obvious allusion to the Salmoxis legend is to be found in the scholium to a passage in Lucian where the direct statement is made that Trophonios retired into an underground room (employing almost the identical Greek words which Herodotos applied to Salmoxis) and there starved himself.

It has long been evident to scholars that the Trophonios cult hinges not so much on the consultation of an oracle (nor on any healing by incubation) as on the mimic descent of a living person to the underworld of the dead and his return thence to the upper-world of the living. It is therefore an immortality ritual. However, I do not think that the connection with Thracian Salmoxis has been properly emphasized; yet it is transparent and, in my opinion, certain. Not merely is the consultant symbolically consigned to the warder of the dead, even as the messenger was dispatched to Salmoxis; but he imitates in his action Salmoxis himself, who feasted, then fasted, then slept in an underground chamber as though dead, and finally returned to life and the light of the world of men.

If ever there was any taint of human sacrifice attaching to the Trophonios cult, it had entirely disappeared; but we are entitled to wonder whether a more sinister practice had not found its way elsewhere into Greece. For there were sites and observances—in Arcadia, Attica, Thessaly, at Patras, on Tenedos—where human victims were vaguely remembered or darkly hinted at; and usually there is in these some element of myth or rite to lead us back to the cult of the bear. The most sinister spot lay in Arcadia, the country which took its name from the bear folk, the Arkades, whose eponymous ancestor was Arkas (a transparent bear name), son of Kallisto, the she-bear divinity. On the highest peak of the land, on the summit of Mount Lykaion, practices continued into classical times, of a sort to trouble more enlightened minds. But so reticent were they on these dubious rites that it is difficult for us to speak about them with much assurance. Says Pausanias, who had visited the spot: "They make sacrifices on the altar in a manner not to be told: I had no wish to meddle in the details of that sacrifice. Let it be even as it is and as it has been from the beginning." In spite of his obvious reluctance, he tells us several precious things: how no mortal may ever enter the sacred enclosure of Zeus Lykaios; whoever does so will die within the year; nothing within the precinct, man or beast, casts a shadow; the hunter who drives his quarry within its boundaries does not follow it in, but waits for it to emerge; when it does so, he perceives that it has lost its shadow. This last detail explains, of course, why it is doomed to die. The shadow is the soul, the incorporeal *alter ego*. Whatever has lost its shadow has lost its soul: it is a *revenant* from among the dead. What is the beast which the hunter drives within the dreaded precinct and dares not follow in? An old fable, written down in late classical times, recounts that Lykaon served his own grandson Arkas for Jupiter to eat; the child, having somehow survived this uncomfortable experience, was reared to manhood among the Aetolians, and there, while hunting, espied his own mother Kallisto roaming the woods as a bearess. Not recognizing her (as who would?), he pursued her into the precinct of Lycean Jove (I fear that Hyginus was weak in his geography: it is a long run from Aetolia to Mount Lykaion)—"where it is the law of the Arcadians that whoso enters must be put to death." Rather than permit so sad an issue, Jupiter set them both amid the stars, Kallisto becoming the Great

Bear, "which some do call the Wain" and we today still more prosaically dub the Dipper.

By the time that a prehistoric animal cult has turned into a nursery fable with metamorphoses into constellations, it has pretty thoroughly disguised its origin and meaning. The story is told in various ways and its primal connections are not always observed. Kallisto is properly the daughter of Lykaon, who may sacrifice any child on the altar of Zeus in lieu of serving up his own grandson to the god at banquet. But Kallisto is regularly changed to bear shape *before* she is set in the sky as a constellation, so that her animal nature is not merely an astronomical equation; and being a favorite companion of Artemis, whom no one should doubt to be, among many other things, a bear divinity,* Kallisto is probably nothing more than an epithet of the goddess herself. The kernel of the whole myth is this: Kallisto-Artemis, the she-bear, is the local Arcadian divinity; Arkas, the bearchild, is sacrificed at a feast of the clan; mimetically, in his memory, a human child is slain at the altar of Lykaios. That this child should be the oldest son of the priest-king does not perhaps follow unequivocally from the story, but is suggested by certain analogies to be discussed a little further on.

Before we leave this site, we should not fail to remark that the local priests on Mount Lykaion were weather magicians. In time of drought an oak branch dipped into a sacred spring could breed a raincloud from which storm would spread.

In Attica also there are traces of a bear cult centering around Artemis, who here carries the cult name of Brauron. In her honor Athenian maidens of proper age and kin dressed themselves in yellow-brown robes and presented themselves as bears to be enrolled in the clan. Was it an aboriginal or a mimic sacrifice of one of these, perhaps the priest-king's daughter, that produced the story of Iphigeneia, the year's fairest product which her father

* As her very name *perhaps* implies by its likeness to ἄρκτος and to the Celtic bear-goddess *Artio*.

owed as due to the Brauronian goddess? At any rate, there were those in antiquity who insisted that the sacrifice was not held at Aulis, but at Brauron in the Artemis precinct, and that when the goddess snatched away Iphigeneia from under the knife it was not a hind but a bear that was found upon the altar.

In northern Greece—around Orchomenos and in southern Thessaly,—in the legends of the ruling house of the Aiolids, the penetration of the Salmoxis cult is singularly plain. Among the seven sons of Aiolos were Salmoneus, Athamas, and Sisyphos; and to each of these some aspect of the legend or of the cult ceremonial attaches.

Who has not heard of Salmoneus, most impious of men, who dared assume even the title and privilege of Zeus and imitated thunder and lightning by driving a chariot of echoing bronze caldrons, while he hurled lighted firebrands against the sky? But who can fail to recognize in this seeming impiety a practice of weather magic virtually the same as that of the votaries of Salmoxis in Herodotos, who "shot arrows at thunder and lightning in heaven and defied the god, maintaining that the only god was their own"? But we have no means of discovering whether the initial identity in the two names Salmoneus and Salmoxis is anything more than a deceptive freak of chance.

For Athamas the case is more obscure, since the celebrated story in Herodotos tells us too little, and that little is ambiguous. The Persian king Xerxes on his southward march through Thessaly came to Halos, and there he was told the local legend of the community banquet hall from which the eldest son of the line of Athamas was ever excluded under penalty of death by sacrifice. Yet many of those under this fearful ban persisted in returning to their native land after having previously fled from it and, being apprehended within the forbidden hall, were garlanded with fillets and led out in procession as victims to be sacrificed. But why should anyone threatened with such a fate have to flee his native town rather than merely be so prudent as not to set foot within the forbidden building? Or, having once escaped the country, why should he later be so foolish as to return? Or having returned, what perversity could have led him to his death by seeking entrance into the hall? If we reflect that there are here all the elements of the Salmoxis legend—the public banqueting hall, the secret disappearance of the chief performer, his return after a period of time, his reappearance in the very place from which he had vanished, and (incoherently telescoped into a single *dromenon* with this sacred legend) the sacrifice of the god's representative—we shall be entitled to suggest that the Salmoxis cult is behind this otherwise inexplicable performance.

The taint of human killing clings close to wretched Athamas, who in the legend sought to slay his eldest-born by his first wife, in madness murdered another child, and would have slain still another, Melikertes, had not his mother Ino leaped with it into the sea. The mother survived, to meet us again in the Odyssey as the hero's rescuer from drowning; but the child succumbed, being either drowned and washed up on the Corinthian isthmus or carried thither on dolphinback. On the latter supposition one would have expected him (like Arion) to have survived his experience; yet, whether dead or sleeping, he was hidden away on the Isthmus by his uncle Sisyphos. For some reason his name became altered in disaster: drowned as Melikertes, he was worshiped as Palaimon. It was commonly believed that the famous Isthmian games were founded in his honor, even as they were celebrated near his sanctuary.

Greek myth often degenerates into such rationalized anecdote that it will tell us nothing, while cult practices and ritual, being more tenacious and less liable to corruption, may still preserve the original significance. So it is with Melikertes-Palaimon at the Isthmus. From Philostratos we discover that his cult was chthonic and that therefore he had nothing to do with the sea beyond his chance association with the lord of the Isthmus, Poseidon. His cult names might suggest our bear cult, since Palaimon should mean "wrestler" or, perhaps, "crafty," while Melikertes is the "honey-eater," as readers of Homer who remember their Greek can attest (*keirein* in both Iliad and Odyssey having the meaning of "eating greedily," as well as the more common sense of "cutting" or "shearing"). Now "honey-eater" is still the universal nickname (or better, taboo name) of the bear in all the Slav languages; and I do not doubt that the mysterious other name of Salmoxis which Herodotos gives as Beleizis (*not* "Gebeleizis," as most editors in defiance of good manuscript authority insist on spelling it),* merely illustrates what Stephanos termed "the barbaric change of B to M," which Kretschmer has established for Thracian names, so that its "barbaric" original form of "MELEÏZIS" could represent some variant of "honey-eater" precisely equivalent to Greek Melikertes. If we distrust such etymologizing as based on wishful semantics and precarious phonetics, we have only to visit the so-called tomb of Palaimon on the Isthmus to discover a setting by now familiar to us.

"Within the enclosure," says Pausanias, "there is on the left a shrine of Palaimon, within which are statues of Poseidon, Leukothea [Ino], and Palaimon himself. Next there is another room called the *Adyton* [i.e., not to be entered], the descent into which is underground; and here they say Palaimon lay hidden."

Who is the Honey-eater who lies hidden in an underground chamber and is worshiped as a chthonic hero, a lord of the dead? Who but Salmoxis the Bear?

His close connection with his uncle, the Aiolid Sisyphos, encourages us to look more closely at this colorful and picturesque figure, for whom the modern students of mythology have suc-

* The *ge* belongs to the preceding word which it "italicizes." For precisely such a grammatical (and logical) use of the particle, cf. Hdt. VII. 152 ἐγὼ δὲ ὀφείλω λέγειν τὰ λεγόμενα, πείθεσθαί γε μὴν οὐ παντάπασιν ὀφείλω. Very good MSS (A and B) omit the γε and read βελεῗζιν only.

ceeded in doing so little. His name has been interpreted as a strengthened form of *syphos* which (to judge from Homeric *a-syph-ēlos,* "foolish") may stand as the Aeolic equivalent of the common Greek word for "wise." "Very wise" he seems indeed to have been in the eyes of the ancient poets: Homer calls him "most cunning," Hesiod "of shifty plans," Pindar "shrewdest in devices," Alkman "much-knowing" (a veritable Odyssean chain of epithets!), and there even was a verb, to "sisyphize," meaning to behave like a thorough rascal. Established tradition was to pair him with Tantalos among the great sinners undergoing eternal punishment in the underworld; and so indeed he already appears in the Odyssey. Yet his crime was not heinous, and his punishment seems illogical. One cannot help wondering how so curious a penalty as that of rolling an elusive boulder up a mountainside was ever devised or why it was imposed upon one whose offenses were variously listed as revelation of divine plans—*deorum consilia hominibus publicavit,* says Servius—and worsting death. Both of these accomplishments belong to Salmoxis, the prophet of the changing seasons, the hibernating visitor to the land of the dead.

As an arch-rogue, clever, intriguing, deceptive, Sisyphos is one of that company of master thieves whose roster includes Odysseus and his maternal grandfather Autolykos, Trophonios with his comrade Agamedes, and traces its spiritual (and often its physical) ancestry to Hermes, the god of thievery. Sisyphos boasted that he could escape death; but how he made good this boast is not uniformly stated. One account maintains that he put Death in chains and held him prisoner until the war-god Ares freed him. Naturally, with Death thus helpless, no men any longer died; and the gods had to interfere. Another version recounts that Sisyphos died and descended to Acheron, but persuaded Hades to allow him to return to the upperworld to arrange for the requisite funeral rites for his own demise. (Let us not fail to note, however irrelevant it may here seem, that this was also the pretext which took Odysseus back from the land of the dead to Circe's isle, that he might bury properly his luckless comrade Elpenor.) Sisyphos had slyly instructed his wife to omit the requisite libations at his grave; but, once safely home, he lingered in the upper air so long that not until old age overtook him could he be compelled to retrace his steps into the kingdom of darkness. (Again we are reminded of Odysseus, who returns from the land of death to live out his normal life, and whose main topic of conversation with the underworld prophet Teiresias is the ultimate manner of his own natural death.) Should we be surprised that there are similarities between Sisyphos and Odysseus, when we discover that (Homer to the contrary) Odysseus was Sisyphos' own son?

No one would have suspected this from reading the Odyssey. But Homer dislikes scandalous tales and expurgates everything that offends his sense of propriety. Despite the eminently respectable parentage through Laertes, everyone in classical times seems to have known and accepted the story that Odysseus' mother Antikleia, on her way to become Laertes' bride, was waylaid by the rascally Sisyphos, and that the only son of the marriage was really his, the intruder's. Odysseus was referred to as the son of Sisyphos in one play by Aeschylos, in two by Euripides, and in no less than three plays by Sophokles. Nor is there the slightest reason for branding the tradition as an Attic or post-epic fabrication.

But we were tracing the resemblances between Sisyphos and Salmoxis. The Corinthian epic poet Eumelos reported that, although Sisyphos was buried on the Isthmus, not many even of his contemporaries could say where. So did Salmoxis make for himself a secret underground chamber in which he might lie hidden, unknown to his fellow countrymen. According to Eustathios, Sisyphos' death was merely an exaggeration of his deliberate temporary disappearance. Here, beyond dispute, is direct association with the Salmoxis pattern. But alas, the worthy but rather tedious bishop of Salonica has not the authority on which an entire case should rest! Because of Sisyphos' mastery over Death, no men died. So also in the Thracian cult those who witnessed the return of Salmoxis from among the dead believed that they too should not die. Sisyphos, in Servius' phrase, announced to men the plans of the gods: Strabo records that Zamolxis was "competent in reporting matters divine." A scholiast on the Iliad quotes Pherekydes (always a most interesting and valuable source for myths) to the effect that when Sisyphos, after having once escaped from the underworld, died a second time, a stone was set for him to roll, "so that he should not run away again." Here perhaps is the true and logical explanation of the great boulder. Was it merely something to block his escape, something that fell back into place and held him prisoner as often as he tried to roll it aside?* Presumably we shall never know; but such a suggestion would fit a pattern and forge a link in a chain of peculiar circumstance. The pattern is a folk tale, and the circumstance is the mysterious connection which the house of Odysseus has with the race of the bear.

Says Telemachos, "God made our line a lonely one, with only

* A great stone was associated also with the Tantalos legend, which combines Salmoxian traits from Lykaon and Sisyphos. Tantalos strikingly resembles Lykaon in serving up his oldest son at table for the gods to eat, an act which without too much suspicion of rationalism may be explained as a reminiscence of the rite of sacrifice of the eldest-born. The punishment of Tantalos may derive from his underworld connections, the threatening boulder above his head being identical with the rock which held Sisyphos prisoner, and the elusive food and drink being a folk-tale deformation of the hibernating fast with complete abstinence from water and nourishment, which always impresses the bear votary (cf. Epimenides!). According to some of the versions of the myth, Tantalos begged the gods for a life like theirs (i.e., aspired to immortality), betrayed divine secrets (like Sisyphos), and stole nectar and ambrosia from the gods to distribute among his friends (i.e., possessed some secret of immortality which he could confer on his followers). If Tantalos was proverbial for his wealth, so was Salmoxis accounted rich and prosperous; but such details are not to be stressed, any more than the occasional late tradition that made Tantalos a king in Sisyphos' town of Corinth. That he is paired with Sisyphos in the Odyssean underworld may be indicative that the two figures are doublets; but it may equally well mean nothing. Tantalos is certainly a highly confused, as well as very old, mythological figure. As such, he cannot be more than superficially connected with the Salmoxis cult, in spite of certain notable resemblances.

son begotten of only son, from Arkeisios to me." And Eumaios the swineherd remarks that if the suitors succeed in their murderous ambuscade of Telemachos, "the tribe of Arkeisios will vanish nameless from Ithaca." Why was descent thus traced from this ancestor? And who was this Arkeisios who headed the family line of Odysseus. The name is a metrical variant of an adjective meaning "ursine, bearish." Thus, the cave on Mount Ida in Crete, where the infant Zeus was nourished by bears, was known as the *arkesion antron* or "bear cave." Used of a man, the adjective is probably intended as a patronymic and means "Bearson." So, at any rate, Greek legend explained it. The story is quoted from a lost work of Aristotle:

Kephalos,* being childless, consulted the oracle at Delphi, which informed him that the first female he might meet after leaving Apollo's shrine should be the mother of a son to him. But the Parnassian trails were empty of human beings and the first female which Kephalos encountered was a she-bear.† The child of that mating was Arkeisios, the Bearson, and he was the grandfather of Odysseus.

If Sisyphos by any chance is Salmoxis, the episode in which he waylays Antikleia and begets Odysseus is merely a variant of this same story, with the sexes reversed and the bear for father instead of mother. The legend of the bear which carries off a woman to his lair and begets a human son is extraordinarily widespread, even as the cult of the bear is one of the most widely diffused of all primitive ceremonials. From Finland and Lapland across the whole of Siberia to the Japanese islands, through Kamchatka and across Bering Strait, across Red-Indian North America to Labrador and Newfoundland, in a vast belt of many thousand miles, there has been traced a bear ceremonial of essentially identical

* Son of Deion of Phokis, another brother in the family of Salmoneus, Athamas, and Sisyphos.

† With this should be read also the modern folk tale from the region of ancient Dodona (J. G. von Hahn, *Griechische und albanesische Märchen,* II, 72 ff., Nr. 75) discussed on page 49 of Bernhard Schweitzer's *Herakles.*

form and content.* Probably because of his plantigrade habits, his erect gait, his swinging arms, his human footprint, the bear seems half human. In consequence the fable everywhere arises that one of his parents was a human being. Thus Frazer records of the east-Asiatic Aino (who, as we have seen, are bear devotees) that they "have a legend of a woman who had a son by a bear; and many of them ... pride themselves on being descended from a bear." In the Odyssean swineherd's phrase, they also would claim to be of the Arkeisian clan!

Homer, of course, would never have told such an unseemly story of a hero's origin; and the closest reading of the Odyssey gives not the slightest encouragement to any supposition that Homer even knew of these ursine associations. He never mentions Odysseus' sister Kallisto, who has the same name as the sacred she-bear of the Arcadians. He never mentions his son Arkesilaos, whose name in the form Arkesilas stands to Arkesios much as *arktylos* to *arktos,* or *arkilos* to *arkos:* in short, is a perfectly good word for "bearson cub" or bear cub—though we hasten to add that it also was a perfectly reputable human name worn by many without an ursine taint! Homer never mentions that Odysseus was really not born in Ithaca at all, but in Boeotian Alalkomenai†

* Consult particularly A. J. Hallowell, "Bear Ceremonialism in the Northern Hemisphere," *American Anthropologist,* XXVIII, 1926, 1–175. Much of this is already to be found in Frazer's *Golden Bough.*

† It seems to be very generally assumed that the hero Kephalos, indigenously Attic, was extraneously and therefore erroneously attracted to Odysseus' ancestry because his name obviously suited him to become the eponymous ancestor of Odysseus' people, the Kephallenes. I think this puts the matter exactly the wrong way round. Through his father Deion—brother of Salmoneus, Athamas, and Sisyphos—a legendary Kephalos is firmly attached to Phokis. The Attic Kephalos, eponym for the Attic deme of Kephale and the Attic clan of the Kephalids, may or may not be a distinct figure later identified with the Phokian. But in either case the Phokian Kephalos remains; and he is intimately allied to the house of Odysseus, since (Pherekydes *apud schol.* Od. 19, 432) Deion had a daughter Philonis, on whom Hermes begot Autolykos, so that on both sides of the house Odysseus descends from Deion the Aiolid. True, Kephalos is not always given as the father of Arkeisios; but on the contrary side of the argument there is not the slightest supplementary evidence outside of Homer to attach Odysseus to the Kephallenes of the Ionian Islands. We must, consequently, accept Phokian Kephalos as a proper ancestor of Odysseus and ascribe to the easy equation between Kephalid and

in the Thracian enclave, not ten miles away from the sanctuary of Trophonios—just below which, incidentally, Pausanias saw the grave of another (or was it really the same?) Arkesilaos.* He does not hint at the oracular functions of Odysseus, which we know from Lykophron and his commentator to have been perpetuated in Acarnania. And he presumably would have made nothing whatever out of the parallelism of the following passages taken from wholly unrelated authors discussing seemingly utterly unrelated topics:

Says Strabo in his account of Zamolxis,

> Thereafter he took over a cavernous spot from which everyone else was excluded; and there he abode, seldom encountering† those of the outside world.

Says Plutarch in a little-read essay,

> Some say that the Etruscans have preserved a tradition that Odysseus became by nature very sleepy and on this account very difficult for people to speak to.‡

A more direct connection between Odysseus and Salmoxis has already been suggested by our peculiar interpretation of the legends attached to his physical father, Sisyphos. Yet, if only

---

Kephallene the transference to Ithaca (which, because it is already in the Iliad, can hardly be attributed to the author of the Odyssey). Similarly, the supposed town of Alalkomenai on Ithaca probably never existed there. The tradition that Odysseus was born in (Boeotian) Alalkomenai being ineradicable, a place of like name was arbitrarily assumed for Ithaca.

In the Prokris legend (accessible as far back as Pherekydes) Kephalos vanishes for eight years in order to test his young wife's fidelity, returns to her rich and unrecognized, wooes and wins the unsuspecting woman, only to reveal his true identity in final reconciliation. Who will dispute that here we have a variant of the same story out of which the Odyssey was evolved? That it should have been told of Kephalos adds one more unbreakable link in the chain between him and Odysseus.

* He is identified with the Boeotian leader (Iliad II. 495) whom Hector slew (XV. 329); but since his father is named either Areilykos (*schol. ad prim. loc.*) or Archilykos (Diod. iv. 67) (cf. the Arkesilaos son of Lykos in Hyg. *fab.* 97) the presence of the mysterious final component of Autolykos, detectable perhaps in Olyxes (?) and Samolxis (??), seems to claim him for the Odyssean clan.

† *σπάνιον ἐντυγχάνοντα τοῖς ἐκτός.*

‡ *δυσεντεύκτου τοῖς πολλοῖς.*

etymological speculations were not so hazardous, an even closer connection might be found in the hero's own name. The form which Homer gives is a deformation along the lines which the Odyssey explores in the painful pun by which his grandfather Autolykos justifies his namegiving of his new grandson. But in classical Greece grandfathers should name the oldest son of an oldest son after themselves. And this is probably what he did. For the evidence from early Greek vases, the Latin variant *Ulixes,* and the existence of a clan of *Olisseidai* at Argos, all go to show that the name was originally something like *Olixes* or *Olyk̑ios.* If the latter, then Aut-olykos bestowed at least part of his name on his grandson; if the former, there may be some connection with Sam-olxis, even though the philologist De Lagarde was no doubt mistaken in interpreting the latter part of the deity's name as equivalent to "bear."*

It is unwise to obscure the issue with etymological uncertainties. Yet the bear names cluster so close about Odysseus that it would be mere blindness or obstinacy to overlook their clue. That clue must by now be obvious. The central theme of the sacred legend of Salmoxis, as a Greek audience rationalized it and retold it to Herodotos, with its distant homecomer with his treasure, who feasts the chief citizens in a great hall, who disappears unexpectedly and is given up for dead, who sleeps in an underground

* If -ολξις echoes any animal at all, I should much prefer a connection with Russian *volk̦,* German and English *wolf,* Albanian *ul'k̦,* Lettish *vilk̦s,* Old Pr. *wilk̦is* (Walde-Pokorny, *Vergl. Wörterbuch d. indogerm. Spr.,* p. 316 *s.v.* u̯l̥qᵘos), and assume *Sam-olxis* to be a compound of the type of *Beo-wulf.* Unfortunately, the lack of etymological information on any cognates for Greek σίμ–β–λος (and σμᾶνος ?), "bee swarm," "beehive," makes any closer identification purely imaginary. *"Es wäre recht schön"* if Beowulf of the Gautar and Geats were merely a Norse transference and reidentification of Samolxis of the Getai!

There appears to be some deep-seated contamination among the Indogermanic words for wolf, fox (and bear ?), perhaps due to taboo or to an undifferentiated generic epithet. Hence the trouble with Lykaon-Kallisto-Arkas on Mount Lykaion, where the bear and not the wolf is worshiped, the "wrongly" formed words *Lyk̦aios* and *Lyk̦osoura,* and the confusion of the disappearing bear votary with a werewolf (Pliny *N.H.* viii. 81–82). So Beo-wulf is ursine, not lupine.

chamber (but perhaps has frequented the underworld of the departed), who suddenly returns to the amazement of all—does not this supply the thematic material also for the Odyssey?

I assume that the Salmoxis cult was brought into central Greece in very early times by immigrant Thracian tribes and that this explains the growth and persistence in that locality of a story similar to the one which Herodotos heard from the Greeks settled on the Black Sea. This explains also why the true home of Odysseus is the Thracian enclave between the Copaic basin and Parnassos and why classical art always represented him as wearing the conical felt cap of the Thracian nobleman. The near-by Minyans of Orchomenos would have learned these sacred legends and preserved and transmitted them in rationalized Greek form. The impiety of Salmoneus, the murderous propensities of Athamas, the underworld adventures of Sisyphos would all be myths based on Salmoxis rites or sacred legends. The seemingly fantastic ritual of Trophonios would be a particularly clear conservation of the Salmoxis cult with its central theme of death and resurrection. But I grant that otherwise (and perhaps precisely because it was not truly Hellenic but a foreign import) the shaggy sleeper in his cave left little impress on Greek religious thought. I find him clear and unmistakable in only one other good Hellenic figure—the Cretan sage, Epimenides. Of him it is recounted by Diogenes Laertius that, though a Cretan, he did not look like one because of his pendant hair. One day, while looking for a lost sheep, he fell asleep at noon in a cave,* only to wake up fifty-seven years later. Emerging, he continued to look for his sheep and thus wandered back to his village, wondering why everything looked unfamiliar (rather like Odysseus waking up in front of the cave on Ithaca and failing to recognize the old but by now unfamiliar landmarks). It is easy enough to decide who this Cretan Rip Van Winkle was. After his amazing slumber he was

* The ἀρκέσιον ἄντρον ?? Max. Tyr. (16. 1) says ἐν τοῦ Διὸς τοῦ Δικταίου τῷ ἄντρῳ.

considered to be under divine protection, and men even sacrificed to him as to a god because of his prophetic foreknowledge. He had a queer gift of taking a minimum of bodily nourishment which caused in him no bodily disturbance or action. He was never seen eating. His soul went in and out of his body at will, and he pretended that he had returned to life* many times. However, there were those who maintained that he had not really been asleep at all, but had merely become a temporary recluse, putting in his time gathering herbs and roots. If the Greek was compelled to humanize his divinities and anthropomorphize his cult animals, could he possibly have supplied a more detailed or better-characterized description of the sacred hibernating bear?

But, in general, the great immortality cult which the European Getai and Daci professed into Christian times did not succeed in capturing the Greek imagination or intruding itself into the major Greek ritual. If Eumolpos and his Thracians, who, according to Strabo, held Attica in early times and were traditionally the originators of the immortality cult of the Eleusinian mysteries, ever taught the worship of Salmoxis, the pre-Greek mother goddess must have won the struggle and displaced the bear, for we never hear of him in Eleusis. Nor is this altogether surprising. Since the proper homeland of the bear cult appears to be the northeast-European forests, it could hardly have ever been indigenous in Mediterranean lands where the bear is an uncertain hibernator, was never very conspicuous, and was of no economic importance as food. If such a cult, once introduced, survived at all in Greece, it was only in such peculiar practices as those of the Trophonian oracle or the sacrifices to Zeus Lykaios, or still more uncertainly in men's minds as an Aeolid myth or, at last, an epic poet's story.

One final aspect of the cult has not been mentioned.

The bear, who sleeps as though dead, belongs among the dead

* ἀναβεβιωκέναι, hence *not* reincarnation as in Plato's myth of Er.

and thereby becomes one of the lords of the underworld. Trophonios attains this stature; Melikertes-Palaimon approaches it; Salmoxis, to whom messengers are sent by slaying, must surely dwell amid the departed and, since he is the only god, must be supreme among them. In an Etruscan fresco at Corneto the enthroned Hades wears a wolfskin headdress; but in a similar scene at Orvieto this seems carefully distinguished as a bear's head; and on a sarcophagus from Chiusi with an underworld scene where Charun stands at the portal with his hammer, an unmistakable bear looks out from within the gateway of death.* Latin classical literature, with its deference to Greek tradition, depresses Orcus, the underworld demon, to a mere place name; but he reasserts himself later to become the modern Italian word for monster and (I do not doubt) the parent of our word "ogre," since Death is the insatiate devourer of men.

In the extreme geographical confines of Latin speech in northeast Italy, the influence of the prefixed indefinite article has changed *un orco* into *norco,* while the definite article has similarly bred *lorco;* and where German speech impinged on Latin, these have produced the *"Nörglein"* and the *"Lorgen"* of the southern Tyrolese peasantry. One has only to listen to the behavior and appearance of these demons of popular tradition to know at once who these descendants of Orcus are. For they look like huge hairy men, have claws and sometimes even tails, and they live in hollow trees, holes, and caverns; they are clownish rather than evil, and may be caught and overpowered and kept captive; one meets them coming out of the woodland in early spring, and the encounter foretells the proper time for plowing and for sowing.

Mannhardt, to whom I owe this record, thought that these wild men of the woods were merely the spirit of the forest, Silvanus; yet surely it is apparent that they are the woodland bears, which

* There is a similar underworld bear on the Etruscan sarcophagus (also from Chiusi) illustrated in pl. 54 of the *Römische Mitteilungen* for 1930.

have always seemed half human to those who have watched them rear up on their hind legs to snuff and shamble. Like Salmoxis of old, the bear has always been the weather prophet in popular belief, down to our own times. Because he presages by his emergence the return of spring to the wintry world, his cult has obstinately survived through pagan and Christian centuries.

The Orcus who was ancestor of *orco, ogre,* and these more harmless sprites, should consequently have been a bear.* But in this more savage aspect the underworld bear is a demon who feasts on human flesh and whom, because he himself is death, no man can kill—though the strongest heroes may perhaps wrestle with him and put him momentarily to flight.

* As might perhaps have been concluded from his name, if it can possibly be derived from the same hypothetical **orc(s)os* from which both Latin and Greek words for the bear are descended. Greek possesses a shorter form ἄρκος parallel to the longer ἄρκτος.

CHAPTER VII

THE FOLK TALE OF THE BEAR'S SON

THE ODYSSEY affords a classic instance of that favorite device of the storyteller, so familiar to us from the *Thousand-and-One Nights,* whereby the main tale is held up while a new one is narrated by one of its characters. Arrived at the court of Alkinoos, Odysseus regales his Phaiakian audience with a long account of his previous adventures while we must hold in suspense our interest in his actual experiences. If this "story within the story" be isolated, we shall be surprised to find how accurately it parallels the leading narrative of the Old English epic of Beowulf.

Due allowance must, however, be made for the catenary technique of the Homeric version, which destroys nearly every unity of time, place, and character by assigning each adventure to a separate scene, after a specific lapse of time, amid its own set of actors. As Odysseus and his wretched companions journey from place to place and undergo adventure after adventure, the men gradually succumb to the hazards until only the hero himself remains. As a result of this deliberate seriation of the plot, there comes into play a peculiar disjunctive narrative process by which any variant or discarded detail of the story may be reinstalled later as a new and separate episode. For example, Polyphemos and Circe are conceivably identical terms from the point of view of their folklore pattern, but have become differentiated into horrid ogre and lovely witch and in consequence have been accepted and introduced as two totally distinct characters. The same may be true of Polyphemos and the Laestrygons, both of whom are ogres. Since the classical scholar is not conversant with such criteria, he normally and naturally sees no resemblance between the ancient Greek and the medieval English epic. Yet, granted the applicability of the method, an almost identical plot emerges.

In both narratives a king's son with a band of retainers sets sail and arrives in a foreign land where he performs extraordinary exploits. In Beowulf a lofty hall full of meat and drink is visited by a huge monster in human form but of superhuman stature and strength, who seizes, dismembers, and devours one of the hero's men. In the Odyssey almost the same incident recurs, save that a cave replaces the drinking hall, and the ogre is himself the owner and occupant. Neither Beowulf nor Odysseus use their swords or knives against the monster; Beowulf because he scorns to slay him thus, Odysseus because he thinks better of an impulse which would have left him and his men prisoners in the cave. Both heroes maim, but do not immediately kill, their adversary: in Beowulf the ogre escapes mortally wounded, while in Homer (as the catenary technique demands) it is Odysseus who flees, leaving the blinded monster behind. In the Greek poem the scene now shifts episodically to the floating isle of the wind-lord and thence to a new land full of gigantic cannibals. In the Old English poem the scene remains the same, while the villain shifts from the male Grendel to his dam, a monstrous hag who clutches and carries off a warrior. In Homer the monstrous hag is the Laestrygonian queen, huge as the peak of a mountain (almost the identical comparison used of Polyphemos), a thing to shudder at; and again Odysseus loses men to the cannibals. Rather later in the story, a dreadful she-monster who lives underwater seizes and eats more of Odysseus' comrades; and Odysseus arms himself against her, contrary to Circe's warning that the beast was not mortal. Close by, where a great fig tree overshadows the water, the maelstrom of Charybdis opens and lays bare the black sand of the sea bottom. The swimming Odysseus does not descend this whirlpool, but clings to the fig tree while the ship's mast and keel on which he has been floating are drawn down and after long waiting returned to the surface. In a northern setting of even more somber horror dwells Grendel's dam at the bottom of the haunted mere, in an underwater hall, to which Beowulf (who like Odysseus is an impossibly prodigious swimmer) makes his way in full armor through the water monsters that "tasked him hard with their menacing teeth." In a separate incident Odysseus makes his way through a land of eternal darkness into the visible underworld of the dead; and this journey may be set against Beowulf's descent to the firelit hall nearly a day's swim down under the "nicors' pool." But the poems differ in that Odysseus accomplishes no exploit in the netherworld but is frightened off by "green fear" of the "Gorgonian head of the dread monster" (whatever that may mean), while Beowulf brings back with him the huge head of Grendel, which four men "scarce could carry on swaying spear."

Is it, then, the same story which has inspired both the Greek and the Old English epic, two poems separated by at least thirteen centuries of time and obvious disparities of language and culture? I think it is, for a reason which will soon become apparent. Yet the dramatic unity which is so strong in Beowulf has been shattered in the Odyssey, where a string of disconnected and unrelated adventures has been substituted for the coherence of time, place and person which might be supposed essential to the primal pattern of such a story. On no possible score could Beowulf have been derived from Homer; and since it is patently preposterous to suggest that the Homeric version derives from the Old English, what possible hypothesis can account for so paradoxical a relationship? The German scholar Friedrich Panzer has shown the way toward a solution by maintaining the highly peculiar (and at first sight thoroughly improbable) thesis that the ultimate source of the plot of Beowulf is a widely known folk tale which he calls The Bearson.* By collating a couple of hundred variants of the story in at least twenty different languages, collected in almost every part of Europe and several sectors of

* Fr. Panzer, *Studien zur germanischen Sagengeschichte,* Vol. I: *Beowulf.*

Asia, Panzer has constructed a master pattern as the nearest possible approximation to an original form from which such various versions might have descended, largely by oral transmission. This master pattern is then compared with Beowulf and the proposal is advanced that it fits so well that we must conclude that the epic poem also is a derivative from this same folk tale, however much decked out in actual historical and geographical circumstance to make it appear as history.

We shall have to leave to the jury of his peers the final verdict whether Panzer has proved his case. Here a very different trial must occupy our attention. We shall take the master pattern of The Bearson precisely as Panzer devised it (with knowledge of Beowulf, and hence perhaps unconscious bias in that direction, but with not the slightest thought of Homer) and apply this to the Odyssey, to show that, whether or not it fits Beowulf, it most certainly fits Homer.

Paragraph by paragraph we shall develop the folk tale of The Bearson, using Panzer's own formulation, and point by point we shall seek (and find) a parallel in the legend of Odysseus.

A wedded but childless woman meets a bear in the forest, is taken to his cave, and remains there to bring forth a son to him. Very exceptionally the child is born of a she-bear and begotten by a man.

It has already been indicated that both of these variants are attached to the Odysseus story, the second specifically in the legend of Arkeisios, Odysseus' paternal grandfather, the first by inference in the postulated Salmoxis nature of Sisyphos, Odysseus' true father.

So strange a child shows traces of his animal origin, is ugly or hairy or has bear's ears.

This detail would have been suppressed by heroic epic as unsuitable and undignified. It is possible, however, that in the original Greek story the bearson did have bear's ears and that this is the real point of the celebrated witticism through which Odysseus escapes from Polyphemos unsuspected by the neighboring Cyclopes. Says Odysseus, "Cyclops, you ask me the name by which I am called. Good, I shall tell you it. Ōtis is my name; so my mother and father and all my comrades call me." The jest of pretending to the name of Nobody—which works out so advantageously when the other Cyclopes come from their caves on the windy heights at the cries of their blinded neighbor and crowd outside his cave to ask "Who is killing you?'" only to get for answer, "Nobody is killing me!"—this jest seems good enough as a ruse against a stupid giant, though it might be doubted whether it is witty enough to satisfy an Ionian Greek audience. Actually, to an archaic Greek ear it concealed still another play on words. In seventh-century pronunciation "ōtis" could have been taken as two words ("no body") or as a single word which was later to be familiar to Xenophon and Aristotle as denoting a bird with long ear coverts, the bustard, while in the closely related form ōtos it was the common name for the long-eared owl. Both words survive in our modern ornithological vocabulary. I imagine therefore that the jest was originally better than it nowadays seems: Odysseus told Polyphemos his boyish nickname "Big-ears," and the giants had only themselves to blame for their misinterpretation. Lest it be thought that I have myself tendentiously invented this subtlety, attention should be directed to the scholiast who insists that Odysseus offers to tell Polyphemos not his "renowned" name (as a later Greek would be tempted, like the modern translators, to interpret the Homeric text), but his "common" name or nickname; that Eustathios similarly asserts that Odysseus had no intention of giving himself the name of Nobody, but was employing a true proper name, comparable to Paris (indeed, were the giant not so stupid, he would have guessed the pun, since Odysseus gives it away by grammatically declining his name wrongly for it to mean "nobody"); and lastly, the Byzantine lexicographer Photios reports that Ptolemaios maintained that "Odysseus had once been called *Outis* because he had big ears."*

All this to save the case for the identity of the Odysseus legend with Panzer's master pattern for the folk tale of The Bearson! We return to the newborn child kept prisoner with his human mother in the cave of the bear.

The bear prevents his captives from escaping, by closing the entrance to his den with some large object, usually a boulder.

This detail, perhaps for its memorable picturesqueness, seems to have survived in transference to Polyphemos' cave:

> But thereat he lifted high and put in place the doorstop;
> Huge it was, such as two and twenty wagons,
> Splendid fourwheeled ones, could not drag from the threshold:
> Such was the rugged stone he put across the doorway.

When the giant goes out again with his flocks for the day,

> Easily taking away the great doorstop, back thereafter
> He put it in place, as one puts the lid on a quiver.

And in this connection it should be remarked that the entire setting of the Cyclops' cavern, in which a great brute keeps humans captive, is possibly only an echo of this feature in the Bearson story.

Mother and son escape from the bear den thanks to the bearson's attainment of sufficient strength to roll the stone aside. (In some versions he kills the bear, his father.) Mother and son return to the human world, where the human husband of the woman adopts the child as his own. He is usually well along in years and cannot hope for other offspring.

Not all of this has left any trace in the Odysseus legend. But the old age of Laertes is frequently stressed, as well as the condition of Odysseus as an only son. Listeners who knew the scandalous story of Sisyphos were well aware that Laertes must have adopted

* In Old Attic *οὔτις* and *ὠτίς* would not merely have been written alike, but pronounced very similarly.

Antikleia's child as his own. In Homer, of course, he passes everywhere as the genuine son of King Laertes. However, even in Homer it is not Laertes but the mother's father, Autolykos, who took the child on his lap and gave it its name. Those who know Greek practice will grasp the implication.*

The child grows up to be prodigiously strong, though sluggish and indolent and generally thought of no account.

Unfortunately, save for the incidents of the boar hunt on Parnassos and the errand to collect payment for stolen flocks in Messenia, we are told nothing concerning the boyhood and youth of Odysseus. But there are two anecdotes in the Odyssey which reveal his extraordinary strength as a grown man: he alone can string the great bow in his halls at Ithaca; and in Phaiakia when he is taunted and challenged by the young men at their sports, he picks up a discus, "larger and thicker and a deal more massive," and hurls it well beyond the farthest mark of the other contestants—very much as his Icelandic counterpart, the outlawed Grettir, appearing in disguise as a stranger at the sports at Heron Ness, is teased into wrestling and proves himself the best of all the company. The Iliad also knows Odysseus as an athlete, especially as a wrestler. In this and in his prodigious power as a swimmer he resembles that other bearson, Beowulf.

Before starting on his adventures Bearson acquires a marvelous weapon which he learns to wield with consummate skill.

In the Odyssey the great bow does not seem wholly due to the exigencies of the plot of the suitor-slaying, but to belong in its own right to the hero. Its history is given in the opening of the twenty-first book, where it is related how Odysseus once went to Messenia to collect a debt for flocks stolen from Ithaca, and there

* If this analysis is correct, "Laertes" should be an invented name, preferably of generic significance like the Kreon's and Kreusa's which fill out the tragic genealogies. Since nothing characteristic or personal is recorded about Laertes, he is without existence in his own right. In his "Labyrinth: eine sprachwissenschaftliche Untersuchung" (*Sitzber. Heidelberger Akad. d. Wiss.*, phil.-hist. Kl. 1932–1933), p. 40, n. 1, Hermann Guntert claims that "Laertes heisst einfach 'Herrscher', genau wie 'Priamos'."

in the house of Ortilochos encountered Iphitos on similar search for missing mares. The two heroes exchanged weapons in token of friendship and thus Odysseus acquired the great bow which Iphitos had inherited from his father Eurytos. This weapon has nothing to do with the tale of Troy; hence Odysseus did not take it with him to the war, but left it at home in his halls "and carried it on his own land." The shooting of an arrow through the line of axheads—a feat not easy to visualize and perhaps not entirely clear to the poet himself—may be a reminiscence of some fabulous proof of skill clinging to the wielder of the marvelous weapon.

Bearson, starting on his adventures, acquires companions endowed with astonishing physical capacities.

There is no trace of a comparable trait in the legend of Odysseus, whose companions are noteworthy for their utterly characterless mediocrity. We know the names of a few of them—Eurylochos, who led the scouting party to Circe's doors and instigated the fatal disobedience on the isle of the Sun; Elpenor, who fell off the roof of Circe's palace, "very fain of the cool air, as one heavy with wine,"—but they are completely undistinguished for any special aptitude. The class which appears in the Bearson stories as creatures of prodigious strength, tearing trees out by the roots, removing mountains, splintering boulders, turning multitudinous mills, diverting rivers and mastering waters, seems uncongenial to Hellenic lore. The other variety, dependent less on brute strength than on supernormal senses and capacities, seems to have been stolen by the poets who sang that other adventurous expedition of the Argo in quest of the Golden Fleece. A famous allusion in the Odyssey suggests that such a poem already existed when the Odyssey was composed and that it enjoyed great popularity.* Perhaps there already had joined the Argo's

* Could this by any chance have been the poem in 6,500 verses, entitled "The Building of the Argo and Jason's Voyage to Colchis," ascribed by Diogenes Laertius to the Cretan Epimenides? Such an epic (because of Colchis) could hardly have been composed earlier than 650 B.C., nor need "Epimenides" have lived much later.

crew and Jason's company such marvelous folk as Lynkeus who could see through rocks and trees, Zetes and Kalais who could fly through the air, Euphemos who could run on the waves, Phaleros whose arrow never missed its mark, Autolykos whose thievery could make every object disappear, Orpheus who could work strange magic with his singing, Polydeukes the wonderful boxer, Castor the swift horseman. If ever the Odysseus legend had any claims to such as these, it seems to have lost them utterly. But it is more than merely possible that they are a later growth to the Bearson story, being attracted from a different type of tale,* as Panzer himself concedes.

The main adventure now follows. Bearson and his companions come upon the House in the Wood. This is frequently sighted from a treetop.

So Odysseus, when he felt himself utterly lost, not knowing where dusk was or dawn, where sunset or sunrise (a strange remark for a Mediterranean sailor!), ascended a rocky lookout and "through dense oak-wood and forest" saw smoke rising from Circe's hall.

The house is empty of owner or occupant, but filled with food, often still cooking on the fire, and with everything in spotless working order. The visitors inspect everything, eat heartily, and go to sleep.

At this point in the Circe adventure, the Odyssey digresses into what might be called the Hänsel and Gretel variant of the House in the Woods with the singing witch; but the magic profusion of food and drink is correctly recorded. The proper Bearson version of the empty house had already been used for the previous adventure with Polyphemos:

Straight came we to the cavern, but found him not within ... So we went into the cave and gazed on all that was there,—baskets well laden with cheeses ... vessels swimming with whey, milk-pails and basins.

* Sc. *Der starke Hans.*

Then we kindled a fire . . . and took of the cheeses and ate, and sat waiting till he should return.

The owner suddenly returns, discovering one of Bearson's companions in charge of the house. He is usually an old bearded dwarf, occasionally a giant, and accosts his visitor politely, but soon turns truculent and manhandles him. One after the other, on successive days, the company has to endure this treatment, until at last it is Bearson's turn.

The Odyssey cannot tell its story in quite this manner, since it must keep all the ship's company together in the cave; wherefore it makes the monster come and go and at every mealtime destroy two victims, with Odysseus correctly and expressly reserved for the last.

True to the folk- tale pattern, Polyphemos enters suddenly and noisily. Catching sight of his puny visitors, he accosts them politely:

Strangers, who are you? Whence sail you the wet ways? Is it for trade, or do you wander at hazard like pirates?

but when he is admonished of the duty of host toward guest, he replies boorishly; a moment later, without further amenity or warning,

he sprang up and laid hands on my companions and grasping two of them together, dashed them like puppies against the ground.

When it is Bearson's turn, he seizes the demon—by the beard, if he has one—and overpowers him. Sometimes Bearson suspends him by his beard from the cleft of a tree; sometimes he cuts off his head or hews off an arm; in any event, the demon recovers himself and makes off to the underworld, whither Bearson follows him by the trail of blood.

Here obviously the Odyssey does not follow the pattern closely. Pursuant to its catenary structure in disconnected episodes, the

House in the Wood is retold in variant form as the Circe adventure, and only then does the hero proceed to the underworld, which he reaches not by following a trail of blood, but by the verbal guidance of the overpowered owner of the House in the Wood. We may deduce, however, that Homer and not our folk tale is here at fault, by observing how badly motivated the *Nekuia* is: Odysseus is instructed by Circe to make the trip to the underworld in order to consult the dead prophet Teiresias about his homeward journey to Ithaca. Yet all the while Circe is far better informed on this subject than he, and it is she in the upper world, and not Teiresias in the lower, who finally instructs him how to cope with the Sirens and pass between Scylla and Charybdis. The curious prophecy which Teiresias makes to Odysseus on the manner of his ultimate death is probably an original element in the legend (we have already met something similar in the story of Sisyphos); but it fills no place in the Odyssey story as Homer tells it, and it seems not to interest its hero in the slightest degree, since on hearing it he coolly answers,

These be, I dare say, threads which the gods themselves have spun; but tell me and speak me true: I see yonder the soul of my mother who is dead.

It was, no doubt, these gaping seams in the composition and this none-too-skillful patching of the narrative which moved Wilamowitz to brand the underworld scene in the Odyssey as an Orphic interpolation. We grant that it fits uncomfortably, even illogically, into place; but if the evidence from the Bearson tale is cogent, we must deny that its incoherences are due to its later origin. Quite the contrary, of all the Odyssean adventures it is the only one, besides those of Polyphemos and Circe, that could not ever have been missing from the story, whose very point and goal it is.

We return to the master pattern of The Bearson.

Access to the underworld is usually down a deep well by means of a rope.

We may perhaps doubt whether the well and the rope represent the original motif. In Beowulf the way to the underworld is through the depths of a dismal pool, which seems confused by the poet with the sea. In the Aeneid there figures a similar body of water, the Avernian lake. In the Grettirsaga the hero descends through a waterfall to a cave behind it—to be sure, by aid of a rope. In the Odyssey there is no echo of such a device unless Charybdis, which lays bare the black sand at the very bottom of the sea, is such a vertical passage to the netherworld, down which Odysseus should have descended with his ship's timbers instead of clinging like a bat to the overhanging fig tree. But Charybdis is strung as a separate bead on the chain of adventures, and so the hero must reach the underworld by a different route up Ocean's stream—perhaps through confusion with that other land beyond the sunset, where dwell the Blessed Ones.

The way to the underworld leads through fire and cold, by wind and water, beset by great darkness, but emerges in a true world beneath, usually adorned with meadows, trees, and flowers.

Here the Odyssey faithfully preserves every essential detail; though perhaps this hardly proves more than a similarity of belief about the netherworld in the general thought of mankind.

There into Acheron flows Pyriphlegethon and Kokytos which is an offspring of Styx.

Here are water and flaming fire. To reach these, Odysseus passes through

the land and town of men Cimmerian, enveloped in fog and cloud. Them beholds not ever the sun shining with his rays, not when he mounts the starry heaven nor when from heaven back to earth he turns; but baneful night is spread over those wretched mortals.

Here, then, is the dense, impenetrable darkness. Beyond are

the groves of Persephone, tall poplars and willows that shed their catkins,

and when the shades come thronging from their underground habitation, they move over meadows of asphodel. Here, then, are the trees and flowered meadows of a world illumined somehow by its own light.

This description of the Cimmerian land has been woefully misinterpreted by ancient and modern commentators alike. Says one of the scholiasts:

These Cimmerians were the Scythians; being nomadic and coming from the western regions of ocean, they sacked Apollo's temple in Delphi; wherefore the poet speaks ill of them, pretending that they were dwellers in darkness.

This is bad enough, but no worse than the modern Black Sea school of Homeric scholars, who, remembering that the historical Cimmerians once inhabited the Crimea (to which they lent their name), proceed to interpret the Homeric passage as a description of the long winter nights of the extreme north. Yet Homer expressly states that the sun rises and sets; merely, it cannot penetrate the fog and cloud with which the country is overlaid—a very different picture from the completely sunless night above the Arctic Circle. Besides, the Crimea is nowhere near the Arctic Circle, being Russia's equivalent to a Riviera and on the same latitude as southern France.

The historical Cimmerians (who raided Asia Minor in the first half of the seventh century and hence not long before the period when we have imagined that the Odyssey was composed) can have nothing whatever to do with Odysseus' western voyaging; hence the importance of looking more closely at the scholiasts and the *variae lectiones* of the manuscripts. These thoroughly challenge the accepted reading: "Aristarchos has *Kerberean*. . . . Some write *cheimerian* (wintry); others, such as Krates, *Kerberian*." Still others offer *Kemmerian*. One of the Florentine codices has *Kimarian*. Since our general MSS authority for Homer is excellent, such falling apart is noteworthy. Obviously, the universally familiar name of the Cimmerians would not thus have been distorted in so many spellings if Homer had originally employed it; whereas, *per contra,* an unfamiliar word, if it resembled Cimmerian, might easily suffer substitution. "Wintry" (*cheimerian*) must similarly be a guess, since had it been the original wording it would have caused no difficulty and been neither challenged nor corrupted. I do not care to offer any suggestion for Homer's true name for these darkness-shrouded guardians of the approach to the world of the dead, but content myself with the suggestion that the fairy tale demanded their presence.

With the entry of the hero into the underworld, the extraordinary resemblance between Odyssey and Bearson ends. In Greek belief, the underworld was a gathering place of the souls of the departed, the once living who had died; for European folk tale, the underworld seems to have been merely another and different world beneath the ground, peopled by demons and monsters, with castles and palaces and dungeons, where there were battles to be fought and adventures to be endured, princesses to be freed, and treasures to be won. In place of these, Homer has had to set conversations with the bloodless shades of the heroic dead and glimpses of those who had sinned against the gods and were undergoing eternal punishment. At most, the princesses whom Bearson frees may find some sort of far echo in the procession of king's daughters which is such a strange feature of the Homeric *Nekuia*. But since there are no battles to be fought and no one to be rescued, the Homeric retelling is left without point or climax. There is nothing for Odysseus to do in the underworld; and so he does nothing. Only a last vestige of something more perilous seems to survive in his final retreat in fear of the "Gorgonian head of the dread monster," lest Persephone send it against him out of Hades.

The great treasure which Bearson wins in the underworld has been transferred to the Phaiakian episode in the Odyssey, where its sudden collection and uncalled-for prodigality ("gifts unspeakably great, such as Odysseus would never have got for himself out of Troy," is Poseidon's irate estimate) put such a strain on the Phaiakian nobles' resources that King Alkinoos hints at a popular levy to recoup them for their enforced generosity! It has more than once been suggested that the Phaiakians themselves are the "gray folk" of fairy lore and that it is unreal fairy gold which Odysseus brings back with him to Ithaca. Truth it is that he hides it all in a cave and appears to forget it completely, and Homer never finds occasion to salvage it for him. If the suggestion is sound, the whole Phaiakian episode may be a surviving representative of Bearson's visit to the underworld; but it has been converted and adorned by promiscuous borrowing from some Argonautic epic, which (as we have seen) had greatly impressed the poet of the Odyssey. Nausikaa is of folk-tale kin to the maiden Medea—the king's daughter, who meets the hero clandestinely and whom the handsome stranger wins by outdoing the native youths in contest. Hence the rather startling conversion of the middle-aged wave-beaten mariner into a Prince Charming through the magic of his fairy godmother Athena. But unfortunately, Odysseus is not Jason, and Penelope waits for him at home; hence that half humorous, half wistful preparing of Nausikaa for marriage and that offer of her hand by her father to Odysseus, who durst say neither yes nor no, but must leave the love-struck girl with little more than a nod of farewell at the last.

There remains one final parallel between the Odyssey and the folk tale of The Bearson.

As Bearson seeks to return from the underworld, the treachery of his comrades delays and all but prevents his escape.

This is, of course, the very device which twice undoes Odysseus' homecoming. Under a favoring zephyr provided by the King of the Winds, the hero has come so close to his native island that he can see fires kindled on the hills. But he is overcome by drowsiness and, while he slumbers, his comrades yield to their curiosity to explore the contents of the leather sack in which they are convinced their leader is conveying treasure. Out rush the winds from the sack and carry the ship back whence it came. Again, on the island of Thrinakia the disobedience of his comrades in killing and eating the Sun-god's cattle leads to the storm in which all the crew perish while Odysseus alone survives by lashing keel and mast together for a raft. So the homeward sailing is ended and not for many a year will Odysseus again behold Ithaca. Shipwrecked on the Ogygian isle, he must keep unwilling company for seven years with Kalypso of the braided tresses. Who she is, does not appear from any searching of the Bearson story, unless her name and her cavernous dwelling betoken still the underworld from which the hero, betrayed by and bereft of all his followers, can find no escape.

In the Bearson story the faithless companions find their way home, bringing the rescued princesses or maidens with them. The variant endings are legion; but a great favorite brings Bearson home in the nick of time to prevent the youngest princess from marrying. He punishes his treacherous comrades and himself marries the princess, with which fortunate triumph the story naturally ends. The obvious parallel with the Odyssey opens the intriguing vista of identifying the suitors with the faithless comrades and Penelope with the rescued princess who is to become a bride for the first time. The suitors' endless eating and drinking is, then, nothing but a projection or prolongation of the marriage feast in which the hero opportunely intervenes. The faithless maidservants who have given themselves to the suitors would be part of the group liberated from the underworld by Bearson and, like his comrades, conspirators in his betrayal; hence the savage severity of their punishment. Penelope would be waiting for

Odysseus, not because he is her husband, but precisely because he is not. Such, at any rate, would be the conclusions from our folklore parallel; but it well may be doubted whether the argument should be pressed to so rigorous an issue.

But with this final speculation eliminated as unsound, the parallel between Bearson and Odyssey is undeniable and unchallengeable. The parallel is there; but what does it prove?

To be frank, in comparative folklore with its lack of written documents and records there are no proofs. There are only probabilities and plausibilities; and these can be evaluated very differently, almost at the pleasure and discretion of every judge who holds the subject in review. But of what weight are probabilities, however highly rated, against the one supreme unlikelihood that a folk tale known over most regions of Europe and some of Asia in modern times was already being told in essentially the same terms in early classical Greece and in such a form that composers of heroic epic could have been tempted to assimilate it to the wholly different genus of quasi-historical saga which dealt with the Trojan cycle?

Are such folk tales really so old? Do they change so little with the centuries? And if so, why are they so persistent? One would hardly class the plot of The Bearson as edifying or even interesting. It is not a very good story; and it is a thoroughly preposterous one. Why should it exert such a power over men's minds?

Only a hundred years ago a seeker for folk tales discovered the story of the priest who mated with a she-bear and begot a heroic son currently told near the site of ancient Dodona.* Was this still the same old tale of the childless man returning from the oracle, that Aristotle had set down? Or had it reëntered Greece from central Europe in modern times? I know no way to answer the question.

At the very edge of the Pyrenees in southern France at Arles-sur-Tech a bear festival was held (until very recently, at least)

* See footnote on page 128.

every year on the Sunday immediately following Candlemas Day. In the middle of the town square a mimic cave was erected—of lath and paper, I presume; in the streets a man dressed in a bearskin terrified the crowd, especially the womenfolk; an appointed victim, dressed in a special costume and for some reason always called "Rosetta," was invariably caught by the bear and dragged to his den, wherein a table was discovered to be decked with cakes and wine. The "bear" politely regaled "Rosetta" with this festive fare, while all the town was invited to attend the "wedding." Here again in contemporary times is the start of the Bearson story; but now it is not told and recounted, but acted out. It is drama; and it is sacred—not because it falls on Sunday or is set with reference to Candlemas Day, but because Candlemas itself falls just six weeks after the sun's deepest retreat into winter darkness, and six weeks is the length of the bear's sleep (both in Aristotle and, more important, in popular superstition). The bear has just emerged from his sleep of death. He is the prophet of the seasons, and his reappearance foretells the return of spring. If he weds on such a day, he has allied himself physically with the spirit of regeneration, and his wedding is no more mysterious than the *hieros gamos,* or mystic marriage, of the *eniautos daimon,* or life spirit, in classical Greek ritual. The Salmoxis cult was a cult of immortality through return to life after the illusion of seeming death, so that its secret was the same as that of all *sacres du printemps,* all spring resurrection festivals in all religions. Is it possible that the Bearson story is only a vulgar retelling in folk-tale terms of a sacred legend, and hence stamped for credence in advance by all the authority of human faith in sacred things? Is not the essence of the Bearson story the struggle with a monster who slays and devours and cannot be killed, even as death slays and devours and cannot be killed, and the descent into the underworld of death, the long abiding there as though lost, and the final triumphant reappearance in the old sunlit haunts of home? And what else than this is the central miracle of the Thracian immortality cult of Salmoxis, which we take to be a southern offshoot of the great bear cult still cherished today? If the cult could survive, its sacred legend might live also and, living, keep alive the vulgar folk tale in which its innermost mystery was enshrined.

How many know that we in America today still make pretense of practicing the old Salmoxis faith? All over western Europe the folklore searcher will still find the Lenten bear, sometimes real, more often made up of mask and straw. He is particularly at home in Slavic surroundings; for example, Bohemia, where the Sudeten Germans willingly took him over from the Czechs. He has become the Lenten bear through the attraction of Carnival with its masks and mummery—not inappropriately, since "Lent" means "spring"; but his own true day undeniably falls some weeks earlier and is not movable like Lent but fixed on Candlemas, the second day of February, when he has ended his winter sleep and emerged from his six weeks of fasting since the winter solstice. In Silesia, Hungary, and Carinthia the feast of Candlemas is still bear's-day in popular observance; and on that precise day (it is maintained) the hibernating bear emerges to see whether or not he casts a shadow: if he sees his shadow, he must retire again for six more weeks of winter. I should imagine that very few, if any, of his votaries understand the significance of this shadow gazing. But if we will think back all the way to the Arcadian bear cult on Mount Lykaion and remember that in that hallowed precinct the entering beast lost its shadow, because the shadow is the soul and the living being which descends into the underworld of death must leave its soul down there (even as Herakles in the Odyssey when he had been transported aloft to banquet among the ever-living gods left behind him in the underworld an *eidolon,* a phantom image of himself stalking like black night "with bow uncased and shaft upon the string")—if we remember all this, we shall understand that the bear emerging from his deathlike winter sleep, having lain as one dead, must have dwelt among the land of shades and therefore should have left his shadow behind him. If he has not done so, if an accusing shadow moves besides him in the wan springtime sunlight, he has not truly been among the dead and he must go back and properly sleep his winter sleep of the full six weeks before he can finally emerge again to announce the rebirth of the world and the imminence of the springtide.

Beyond the Slavic radius, in regions where the bear was not so sacrosanct or perhaps had grown so scarce that his dens were no longer to be found (but as far as my information goes, only on German soil), this same superstition was transferred from the bear to the much smaller badger, which is also a hibernant. German immigrants to Pennsylvania* brought this tradition with them and, in default of badgers, fixed it on the much more plentiful and very bearlike little marmot, the ground hog, whose modern official name of *Arctomys monax* confirms his bearish properties. The memory still survives: jest and make-believe have replaced credulity, veneration, awe, and worship—but still, nearly two and a half millennia after Herodotos' record, we keep, however lightly and ignorantly, some memory of the great immortality cult of Salmoxis and the Thracian bear.

Can we look still farther back into the centuries and behind the mild European brown bear, *Ursus arctos,* catch a glimpse of the fearful *Ursus spelaeus,* the cave bear, who disputed with primitive paleolithic man the precarious shelter of the Central European hillsides, the surly cavern dweller who, like Polyphemos, might return to find puny mortals huddled in terror in the dark recesses of his home? I doubt if such a memory could survive through stretches of time which make Grettir and Beo-

* Cf. E. M. Fogel, *Beliefs and Superstitions of the Pennsylvania Germans,* Philadelphia. American Germanica Press, 1915. (Consult item 1218.)

wulf and Odysseus into folk of yesteryear. Perhaps it is better to think that the bear, as lord of the underworld, can borrow from death terror enough to explain the fearful ogre who breaks into the feast and claims his victim. Death in the midst of life, and some hope of life even after the crushing calamity of death—it is this, if my interpretation is correct, which is the real theme of the seemingly foolish folk tale of The Bearson; and it is this, touching the deepest of all human fears and the highest of all human hopes, that explains why such a story could keep itself unchanged through centuries and captivate an Ionic epic poet in archaic Greece equally with a heroic singer in Denmark or Northumberland or a storyteller in the distant sagaworld of Iceland.

CHAPTER VIII

FACT, FABLE, AND FICTION: THE FINAL VERDICT

"BETWEEN Lengenfeld and Stoffen there lies a waste upland where the Wild Chase is prone to linger as it rages overhead. Not long ago a man from Hofstetten was crossing this particular stretch at nightfall when there came to him out of the distance a sound as of a rising storm; and even while he stood and wondered, the Wild Chase went by in the air above him. Because in his fright he failed to throw himself to the ground [as one always should do when the Wild Chase passes] he was caught up by it and carried off. He was missing for six weeks, during which nobody knew where on earth he was; and his relatives were mourning him for dead, when all of a sudden he reappeared. He himself could not say how or whence he had returned, but seemed completely dazed by his experience. He is still alive; but he neither laughs nor weeps, and sits dumbly all day by the kitchen fire."

This anecdote dates from about a hundred years ago. Being narrated so circumstantially in the matter of time and place and person, it might be thought to be a reasonably truthful record of severe fright followed by amnesia. Perhaps only a folklorist would object that six weeks is the classical duration of the bear's hibernation and that the Wild Huntsmen are spirits from the dead. And perhaps only the classicist (or the public at these lectures) would detect certain echoes—"His relatives were mourning him for dead, when all of a sudden he reappeared." Did not Plutarch write of a consultant of Trophonios, "He remained two nights and a day underground; and just as most people had given him up for dead and his family was mourning him, at early dawn he emerged radiant"? . . . "He seemed completed dazed by his experience . . . and neither laughs nor weeps." Was it not Pausanias who recorded of the consultants of Trophonios that they "often emerged in such a state of terror and bewilderment that it was a long time before they ever laughed again"? Yet we shall not suspect the man of Hofstetten or his chronicler of reading Plutarch and Pausanias!

Even more circumstantially attested is the following memoir by the town clerk of Lucerne in Switzerland, under date of slightly less than four hundred years ago:

"In 1572, on November 15th, a peasant named Hans Buochmann, otherwise Krissbueler, of Romerschwyl, aged 50, personally known to me, disappeared mysteriously. Four weeks later, reliable information reached us that he had been seen in Italy, at Milan. Finally, on Candlemas Day of the ensuing year, 1573, he returned with a bruised and swollen face and without hair, beard, or eyebrows. When the authorities learned of his reappearance they had him arrested and examined, myself being present at the hearing. His sworn statement was to the effect that he had 16 florins on him the day that he disappeared, with intent to pay a debt, but had not found his creditor, so had gone on to Sempach for an errand, stayed there till dusk, had a drink or two, but not too much, and was coming home through the forest when, on nearing the spot where the great battle was fought, he heard a strange series of sounds, at first like a swarm of bees, then like music of stringed instruments, which thoroughly frightened him. He drew a weapon and laid about him in his terror, when suddenly he lost his senses and was caught up in the air and transported to a foreign land where he had never been before. On the fourteenth day thereafter he found himself in Milan, where a German soldier of fortune befriended him."

The contemporary source from which I have translated this account treats the incident medically as a case of what it terms the twilight state in epilepsy, considering the testimony reliable and the event therefore actual. For myself, I cannot quite ascribe it to sheer coincidence that our vanished rustic was snatched away precisely at a spot where the dead must have been thought to lurk and that he turned up again exactly on Candlemas Day, the second of February, the immemorial date for the winter bear's reëmergence. Neither do I blame his alleged loss of hair, beard, and eyebrows on epilepsy. I can only wonder whether he still cast a shadow.

In tracing back into the past the curious history of the Man Who Disappeared, we shall have to pass over such recent and literary versions as Washington Irving's *Rip Van Winkle,* however perfectly it conforms to type, and disregard Coleridge's Ancient Mariner, whose striking resemblances to Odysseus are most simply explained on the assumption that the poem was bred of unconscious memories of early readings in Homer quickened with a lively interest in contemporary Antarctic voyages of exploration.

Safely back in the classic world, we shall note that it was precisely in the year 492 B.C., at the great Olympic festival, that Kleomedes* was debarred from the prize in boxing because he had accidentally killed his adversary, Ikkos of Epidauros. In high ill-humor Kleomedes returned to his native island of Astypalaea and there pulled down a schoolroom on its children by exerting too much strength against a column. Pursued by the enraged townsmen, he retreated to Athena's temple, sprang into a wooden chest and pulled the lid shut behind him, holding it thus against all efforts. When at last the lid of the chest was pried open, there was no one inside. The Delphic oracle, on being consulted, proclaimed the vanished athlete the "last of the heroes." Kindly observe that time, place, and circumstance are attested quite as specifically for Kleomedes of Astypalaea as for Hans Buochmann of Romerschwyl.

* Plutarch, *Life of Romulus,* xxviii. 4; Paus. vi. 9. 6–8.

After once more saluting the sage Epimenides who slept fifty-seven years in a cave, we shall pass to the strange accident which befell Aristeas of Prokonnesos, as recounted in the pages of Herodotos. Here the hero is an Ionian Greek seemingly every bit as genuine a person as Epimenides of Knossos and like him a writer of verse, though of rather a different cast. He dwelt on the Sea of Marmora, and his date is set rather earlier than Kleomedes or Epimenides or the freed slave of Pythagoras.* This Aristeas had composed a travel epic in which he told of being possessed in spirit by Apollo and of visiting a far people, the Issidones, beyond whom dwelt the one-eyed Arimaspians, and beyond these the gold-guarding gryphons, and beyond these the Hyperboreans, Apollo's favorites. But this is not the story. Herodotos comes to it a little later, after explaining that he had himself heard it in Prokonnesos and Kyzikos, where (as men told him)—

Aristeas belonged to one of the leading families. One day while he was visiting a fuller's shop, he suddenly died. So the fuller locked up his workroom and went to inform the next of kin. But even as the news of the event was spreading abroad in the town, there came a Kyzikene from the town of Artake and disputed with those who insisted that Aristeas was dead. "I met him," said he, "coming into Kyzikos and conversed with him!" He clung doggedly to his story, even while the dead man's kin were assembling outside the fuller's shop with a stretcher to carry off the corpse. So they opened the locked room, and lo, there was no Aristeas to be seen, either dead or alive! It was six full years later that he turned up again in Prokonnesos and, out of the

* My earliest candidate for the Man Who Disappeared belongs to the thirteenth century B.C. and the Hittite interior of Asia Minor. Telebinu vanished during the winter, causing a state of death for all things. The eagle, sent in search of him, could not find him anywhere on earth. Finally the bee, sent on the same errand, succeeded in locating him fast asleep as though dead, in a cave. With much trouble she managed to arouse him. At Telebinu's return, life came back to the earth. (Ehelholf, *Keilschrift-Urkunden aus Boghazkoï,* XVII, 1926, Nr. 10. I owe my acquaintance with the story to Picard, *Revue des Etudes Anciennes,* XLII, 1940, pp. 280 f.) I must leave to others' judgment whether the bee and the cave are sufficient to identify this hibernating life spirit with our old friend the bear.

adventures which he had undergone, composed the verses which the Greeks call The Arimaspea. When he had completed these, he disappeared a second time.

There is an obvious resemblance here to our friend Hans Buochmann of Romerschwyl who disappeared with equal suddenness in 1572, was reported as seen elsewhere, was apparently wandering in distant lands, and as unexpectedly returned to his old haunts and habits. We noted that there was a modern suggestion that Herr Buochmann was an epileptic: Aristeas' behavior, too, might be thus explained. Does not Herodotos himself record that he was *phoibolamptos,* and is not this much the same word and notion as epileptic? Under the epileptic seizure, the sudden rigid fit of unconsciousness was mistaken for death by the fuller, during whose alarmed absence the victim might have regained his senses with no clear memory of what had befallen him and, discovering some other exit from the fuller's shop, have wandered off in a state of bewilderment. Out of so simple a medical history there developed so wonderful a tale!

But I doubt if such an interpretation can be correct.

The leading citizen of Prokonnesos corresponds too closely to the wealthy and civilized Salmoxis, the fuller's shop to the secret underground chamber, and the mysterious disappearance, prolonged absence, and unexpected return are of the essence of both stories. As usual, the documentation with name, place, and circumstance is complete; but so was it for Hans Buochmann and the man from Hofstetten. No audience will believe the story of the Man Who Disappeared unless it is thus presented under guise of firsthand authenticity.

We should be utterly at a loss to understand how a variant of the rationalized Salmoxis legend had come to life in Kyzikos and attached itself to an early poet, had not Herodotos proceeded to inform us that he had crossed the track of Aristeas elsewhere, in the western Italic land. There, in Metapontum, he saw a statue inscribed "Aristeas" standing amid bay shrubbery beside the image of Apollo; and he elicited from the Metapontines an involved story about a phantom which had appeared in their midst and proclaimed that he was Aristeas and that they should dedicate an altar to Apollo, along with much else in similar vein. Even so, we of today will not be much the wiser unless we happen to recall that Apollo's prophetic aide was named *Aristaios,* not Aristeas, that he is Vergil's "lord of the bees," that he was a rustic divinity in his own right, presiding over cheesemaking and olive culture and the hiving of honeybees. And unless we track him down still farther, we might fail to notice that he was reared in the Athamantid Plain of Thessaly, that he had Aiolid connections, that he was also a weather prophet, that bear hunters invoked his name, and that once he went to Thrace on a visit to Dionysos and there, after dwelling on Thracian Mount Haimos for a time, disappeared from sight, thereby attaining immortal honor among Greeks as well as barbarians. Aristeas-Aristaios is the honey-eater, the disappearing dweller on the mountains, the Thracian Salmoxis. His name, like Kallisto and Trophonios,* is an honorific or precautionary title, since among bear worshipers the bear's name is uniformly taboo. That is why he is still today "Honey-eater" in all Slavic languages and "Bee-wolf" in the Old English poem. His cult must have been brought to Kyzikos by the Thracians, who seem to have been the earliest settlers of that locality. Shall we be surprised to learn that the Kyzikene territory is redolent of bear? The great headland beyond the isthmus on which the town was situated was called Bear Mountain. Local legend asserted that the infant Zeus had been reared there by she-bears; and the shaggy six-limbed giants of the Argonautic adventure on this same headland are the bears which walk on all fours and have two arms pendant when they stand erect. Bear

* *Trophonios* should be *He-of-the-tropheion* (den or lair)? In his *Ion,* Euripides applies to the Trophonian sanctuary the words σηκοὺς and θαλάμας (fem.) which he uses in his *Phoinissai* of the Theban dragon's lair.

Island is close by. And there is a town Artake and a fountain Artakia, in both of which it is not impossible that the bear name lurks.

Was there ever a citizen of the town with the name of Aristeas, son of Kaustrobios, who wrote poetry about one-eyed Arimaspians and gold-guarding gryphons? I do not doubt that there was such a poem; but nothing is known about its author. Possibly, like so much oral poetry, the Arimaspea was in reality anonymous, and Aristeas was merely the poem's imagined narrator who underwent its adventures and recounted them, much as Odysseus in the Odyssey (also perhaps an anonymous composition!) rehearses his own adventures to King Alkinoos. However, this is none of our affair today. For us it is enough that the rationalized sacred legend of the Thracian bear was not told among Greeks only in the form which Herodotos had learned from his countrymen on the Black Sea and the Hellespont, where it was current of the rich barbarian freedman of Pythagoras, but had so worked its way into local esteem that it could be told of an Ionian Greek by Ionian Greeks in an Ionian town.

The case of Odysseus is not a whit more extraordinary or improbable. He too carries the telltale marks of the Man Who Disappeared. He too had vanished but was reported as having been sighted in foreign parts: the swineherd warns Odysseus that "whoever comes in his wanderings to Ithaca goes and tells his silly tales to my mistress, and she entertains him and asks every detail," since they all profess to have met the missing hero. But the swineherd is convinced that he is dead, and Penelope has come to a similar conclusion. Her son Telemachos refers to him as the one whom the gods made to disappear "as no man ever before." Yet after long years, of a sudden there he is, back again in his native land. He awakes under an olive tree at the mouth of a bee-haunted cave and knows not where he is nor how he has come there.

Perhaps it is disconcerting to have the story attached to a hero of the Trojan War, one whose epic status is equal to that of such great figures as Diomede or Ajax. Yet the character which the Iliad offers us—of stalwart fighter, shrewd counselor, and persuasive orator—cannot be primary or original. Having accepted him among the epic company of heroic saga, the poets of the Trojan War remade Odysseus to their own liking, keeping only the wily thief of the bear stories and the strong-armed wrestler, "broad of shoulder and chest . . . like a thick-fleeced bellwether ram." But the poet of the Odyssey has relied on older and presumably more popular sources and, accepting the Trojan warrior and all the tale of Troy, has yet succeeded in combining with that heroic environment a folk tale rationalized out of the bear legends brought into Greece from more northern lands at some unknown period.

Were it not for the Herodotean accounts of Salmoxis, the slave of Pythagoras, and Aristeas, the wandering poet, and the telltale details in the legend of Epimenides, the wizard, one might well challenge the possibility that a sacred myth based on an animal cult could ever be thus disguised or could succeed in passing over from the category of sacred legend to that of heroic saga. One cannot therefore too closely scrutinize the workings of the rationalistic interpretation which the Greek mind gave to the Getan myth of Salmoxis. Out of the divine teacher and sacred ancestor the Greeks who heard the story had made a barbarian slave who had acquired intimations of immortality from an apprenticeship to a well-known Greek religious philosopher; of his winter den they made an underground room which he had secretly built with his own hands; out of the sacred feast they made a rich man entertaining the leading folk of the town in the town banquet hall; and of his holy mystery of sleep and resurrection they made a clever mundane swindle.

Partly it was ingrained Ionian materialism—for I do not doubt that it was Ionic colonists who evolved the Salmoxis story,—the Greek skepticism toward all pretensions of magic, a deep aversion to the supernatural as the proper explanation of any event, which impelled them thus to rationalize and humanize. But also it must have been the storyteller's instinct for his task, the wish of the narrator to carry conviction and to be believed, which led them to substitute the ready plausibility of everyday experience for the hard improbabilities of the miraculous. It is interesting that Herodotos knew his countrymen too well to show them much credulity; he saw through their well-turned story and perceived that Salmoxis had nothing to do with Pythagoras but was some sort of native barbarian deity.

If we excise from the Odyssey all that is borrowed from the heroic trappings of the Tale of Troy, we shall have a folk tale ingeniously converted into a *novella,* a story of quasi-contemporary human incident. And if in this we disregard all the folk-tale material which we have had under discussion, the Bearson story and every other supernatural event or issue, we shall have a final residue of pure fiction, the poet's own formative contribution to his poem. Such characters as Eumaios the faithful swineherd and his opposite, Melanthios the unfaithful goatherd, as well as Philoitios the neatherd who in turn holds true to his master, or Iros the beggar whom the suitors encourage against the ragged rival newcomer (who is Odysseus in disguise)—all these, who have nothing to do with the folk tale, so strongly resemble the minor accessory characters of Attic drama that we need not hesitate to brand them as pure invention to keep the story moving and enrich its episodic human content. Less certain is Penelope, the heroine. But since the Bearson tale has only a hero and no proper heroine, we may rightly challenge Penelope's claim to be much more than a mythologically available character. Her stratagem of weaving and unraveling an ever-unfinished web in order to put off her marriage to any of the suitors is a motif typical of

Märchen, perhaps suggested by some *Märchen* prototype; yet it seems to have arisen directly out of etymological suggestion (like so much else in Greek thought and fancy), since the initial component of *Pēnelope's* name could not fail to suggest to a Greek ear such words as *pēnē,* the woof in weaving, and *pēnion,* the weaver's bobbin or spool. Save that she mourns for her absent lord and resists the pressure to rewed, she has no active part in the plot and displays few interesting qualities. Thinking back, the reader will remember her only as descending from her upper chamber, where she has been weeping, and standing statuesque and a trifle unhappy in the doorway of the great room where her suitors are gathered. We may even guess how it was that the poet of the Odyssey came to evolve her character in deliberate antithesis to the infamous Klytaimnestra. For the Odyssey talks with needless frequency about the murder of Agamemnon through Agamemnon's unfaithful wife.

At the very opening of the poem, with the high gods in council, Zeus begins from Agamemnon's death at the hands of his wife and her paramour Aigisthos (whose name—completely irrelevant to the plot of the poem—occurs no fewer than twenty times in the Odyssey). A little later, Athena refers to him and how Orestes slew him, in order to incite Telemachos to avenge his father. In the third book, Nestor tells the story at length; in the fourth, Menelaos adds yet further details. In the *Nekuia* the shade of the murdered Agamemnon laments to Odysseus his death through Aigisthos "with the aid of my accursed wife," whom he deliberately contrasts with Penelope:

> But thou, Odysseus, shalt not find death at the hands of a woman, thy wife; for she is understanding and hath care in her heart, even the daughter of Ikarios, wise Penelope.

And finally, at the conclusion of the poem, when the shades of the suitors are herded into the underworld and tell their story to Agamemnon, he cries aloud:

> O happy son of Laertes, wily Odysseus, what a virtuous wife didst thou take thee! . . . The fame of her virtue shall never perish; but the immortals shall make for the earthfolk a delightful song of steadfast Penelope,—not as the daughter of Tyndareus, working evil deeds, slaying her wedded husband; *her* song shall be hateful among men!

There we have the contrast, in explicit terms, as though it were the poet's own final confession of the source of his inspiration.

In the main, therefore, the Odyssey is almost entirely fiction, being an immemorial folk tale rationalized and humanized and heroized and set most persuasively on a western Greek island amid the pigs and goats, the dogs and beggars, the sailors and landsmen, of the archaic Greek world of the late seventh century before Christ.

Even so, in this form, it is not the first time of its telling nor the first place of its setting which we possess in our Odyssey. The poem as we have it implies an earlier state out of which it has been evolved with a shift of scene, due perhaps to deference for the greater authority of the Iliad, which already seems to have known Odysseus as the man of Ithaca.

Wilamowitz was among the first to emphasize the Odyssean references to Thesprotia and Epirus, the coastal region about a day's voyage for an ancient ship working north beyond Ithaca. It is here, in Thesprotia, that the underworld river, the Acheron, flows, and the Acherusian lake is formed, to be joined by the confluent Kokytos, as in Circe's description of the way to the underworld. It should be here, therefore, that Odysseus originally descended to the kingdom of the dead. Not far up this same coast, near Apollonia, Herodotos* still knew of flocks sacred to the sun. It is through Epiros that the way led up to Dodona, where Odysseus was supposed to be lingering; and it is from the Thesprotian coast that he himself pretended to have been conveyed home. It

* IX. 93, with an assigned date of *ca.* 500 B.C. The ἱρὰ ἡλίου πρόβατα were strictly protected by the inhabitants of Apollonia, who punished with loss of sight a careless guardian.

is in the hinterland behind Thesprotia that the scene was laid for those later and final adventures of Odysseus which (perhaps through borrowing from an older poem, the *Thesprotis* of Musaios) were recounted by Eugammon of Cyrene in his epic poem, the *Telegony*.

Still more convincing is the astonishing (and comparatively recent) observation that Odysseus, in describing his homeland to King Alkinoos, if he is speaking of the Ionian Islands at all, is certainly claiming Corfu and not the present Ithaca for his native isle. One has only to glance at the map to see that the island which (in Odysseus' words) "lies low, furthest up the sea-line toward the darkness," while its neighbor islands all lie "very close together, apart toward the rising sun," can only be Corfu, situated at some distance from the compact remainder of the group, whose last outlier it is on the horizon along the sea journey to the West.

Again, the suitors' ambuscade of Telemachos, and Athena's directions for evading it, make absolute nonsense for Ithacan topography. There is no island "in the strait between Ithaca and Cephalonia" possessing a double harbor or large enough to permit outlook from its windy heights. Even if there were such an island, there would still be something fundamentally wrong with the story, since Telemachos' ship apparently sails past the ambush in broad daylight, unchallenged and even unnoticed. Finally, Athena's instructions to Telemachos to "keep his ship far from the isles" on his homeward trip from Pylos is incapable of reasonable explanation. But if the scene had originally been laid in Corfu instead of Ithaca, all the details would become both intelligible and accurate. For there is an island (nowadays and in late classical writers called Paxos) which lies to the south of Corfu on the direct course past the Leucadian promontory to the Peloponnese; it is rocky and bare and runs up to six-hundred-foot ridges swept by the wind, whence there is an uninterrupted view, so that any ship approaching from lower Greece can be spotted from afar; in its single good harbor, thanks to a tiny islet in the mouth, it actually possesses an anchorage with double entrance; and Athena would have indicated to Telemachos the only possible manner of eluding its ward by instructing him to sail by night and hug the mainland, thus "keeping afar" from the little island group of Paxos and its companion Antipaxos. At the end of this run, his ship would have to cross boldly the six-mile strait to the nearest headland of Corfu; but by that time the harbor of Paxos would lie nearly double that distance behind, so that there would be nothing for the baffled suitors to do except to bring their ship home empty-handed. Even if they overtook Telemachos' ship before it finally made the town, Telemachos himself would have been safe ashore and beyond their reach. In such a setting, with Corfu for base and Paxos for point of lookout and concealment, the suitors' plans would have been correctly laid and intelligibly frustrated.*

Nonetheless, most of the Odyssey undeniably demands Ithaca *and not Corfu* for its scene. On the resultant complications with their mutual contraditions are based the arguments for the famous Doerpfeldian heresy of Leukas, a theory which removes a few difficulties only to breed others and leave still others unresolved.

Beyond this inference that an earlier setting on Corfu with its opposing mainland has been violently, but incompletely, adapted

* The legend of the *μαρμαρωμένο καράβι*, the ship turned to stone, is still told at Corfu, being localized along the west coast opposite the monastery at Palaeokastritsa and retold in Christian terms. If the Odysseus story was originally told of Corfu, the Phaiakian ship must have been turned to stone by Poseidon at the start of its homeward journey to Phaiakia. Later, the scene having shifted to Ithaca, the legend was preserved, but its relation to Odysseus' homeland altered. The persistence of this legend in Corfu, where the stone ship was actually to be seen, presumably was responsible for the otherwise preposterous classical identification of Corfu with Scheria, the Phaiakian land. I am not a convinced votary of *Sagenverschiebung;* but it is fairly obvious that when Odysseus the Kephalid assimilated the Kephallenes as his people, his kingdom had to be shifted to Kephallene territory. In fairness, it should be noted that Homer nowhere mentions Kephalos. The nearest approach is in Od. xxiv, where Odysseus refers to his father as Arkeisiades (to which the scholiast observed that Arkeisios was *ἐξ ἄρκτου γυναικός*) and Laertes refers to himself as lord of the Kephallenes.

to a situation some hundred miles farther south on the island whose modern name of *Thiaki* bears testimony to its identity in classical times,—beyond and farther back than this we cannot penetrate, since the documents all were oral and all have perished.*

◇ ◇ ◇

It is time to turn for a final glance at the Iliad.

Apart from the supernatural appurtenances of its central character Achilles, folk tale has left little trace on the carefully humanized drama of the Iliad. Occasional reminiscences from the mouths of the embattled heroes alone offer opportunity for forsaking the unmagical beach of the Hellespont in search of more marvelous scenes. In the mid-field of combat Glaukos sets forth his ancestry to Diomede and narrates the story of Bellerophon. On embassy to Achilles' cabin, Phoinix tells the story of his own youth, and on the same occasion, with an old man's garrulity, proceeds to the tale of Meleager's wrath, "a story of old, and no recent one." Here and there the aged Nestor touches on strange events of the past. It is a scant harvest for so huge an acreage. Yet what is offered is by no means without interest.

It will be remembered that at Halos in southern Thessaly the eldest son in the line of Athamas was always sacrificed if he were caught within the public banquet hall. With this in mind, let us listen to Phoinix in the Iliad, recounting an escapade from his own youthful days

when first I left Hellas of fair women, fleeing a quarrel with my father, Amyntor son of Ormenos, who was greatly angered at me

* Teiresias' curious prophecy to Odysseus in the underworld necessitates some sort of sequel to the original story. Whether or not the cyclic epic the *Telegony* correctly reproduced it, such a second part recounting an inland journey and the hero's death from a wound and his burial in a mounded barrow (implied in the planted oar, traditionally the sailor's tomb marker) has its parallel in the final incident in Beowulf, which differs from the commonplace dragon fight in not being a youthful exploit, but the occasion of the death and burial of the hero in his old age.

because of his fair-haired mistress, whom he ever loved, to the dishonor of his proper wife, my mother. Time and again she besought me to take that mistress away for myself, that the old man might grow distasteful to her. So I yielded and did the deed. And on the instant that my father learned of it, he cursed me mightily and called on the loathed Furies, that never a son sprung of my loins should sit on my knees; and the gods fulfilled his curse, even Zeus underground and awful Persephone.... Then was the spirit in my breast no longer to be restrained that I should frequent the halls of my angry father. Yet my clansmen and my kinsmen that were nigh restrained me indoors with many a prayer; and many fat sheep and crook-footed horned kine they slaughtered, and many greasy swine they seared and held over Fire's flame, and from that old man's wine-jars much was there of strong drinking.

Nine nights they camped all night about me, changing their guards, nor let the fires die, neither under the portico of the well-fenced courtyard nor yet at the entry to my chamber doors. But when the tenth night came on me with its darkness, I broke the close-fitted doors of the room and came forth, and lightly I leapt the courtyard's barrier, unspied by the men on guard or the women-servants, and I fled afar thereafter through spacious Hellas, and I came to deep-soiled Phthia, the mother of flocks.

Obviously, the youthful Phoinix interfered in affairs that were not his own, and well merited his father's angry outburst; yet he takes a contrary view of the matter and persists in most violent resentment against his father, whose house he determines to leave. Why then is he held prisoner there? And what is all the feasting and revelry about? Can we credit (or sensibly interpret) the ensuing situation, where his clansmen and kinsmen hold him behind locked doors while they waste the king's wine cellar and herds, keeping watch through the night with fires blazing before the house, until Phoinix at last breaks out by force and by stealth and so escapes unharmed from this curious captivity? The emotional cause-and-effect runs crooked, and there seems no rational sequence in the events. An erotic motive has been prefixed to some different kind of story. The mother begging the son to seduce his own father's mistress in order that she, the lawful wife, may be rid of a difficult rival, is piquant and most unusual and hence highly successful; but it has nothing to do with the scene that follows. If this introductory episode be dropped, the *novella,* the pointed story of contemporary incident so like in theme to a comedy of manners, disappears and a totally different type of tale remains.

Though the scene of the story is laid elsewhere, Phoinix properly belongs in Phthia, where he ruled the Dolopians—"at the outermost of Phthia," as the Iliad puts it.* But Phthia is also the land in which Halos is situated; and the latter portion of the story which Phoinix tells bears a remarkable likeness to the Herodotean account of the strange customs of Halos.

The father's curse on his son, invoking Zeus of the underworld and dread Persephone to see to it that no children shall ever sit on his knees,—what is this but a euphemism for the extinction of the family line by the death of that son? The high feasting in the hall wherein Phoinix is held unwilling prisoner runs parallel to the town banquet hall from which the victim is led out with pomp and sacrificial ceremony to his death. And the escape from such imminent catastrophe (perhaps with the connivance of his kinsmen gaolers) into the safety of exile is a prominent feature of the Herodotean account. The two stories are at bottom the same. Only, what is generic ritual for the historian has become specific and personal adventure for the epic poet. A cult myth, based on a barbarous ceremonial practice, possibly of considerable antiquity, has made its way into polite epic and been assimilated to the Homeric group of saga stories so skillfully that it is barely distinguishable from the rest of the tale of the Achaeans who fought at Troy.

* Apollodoros and Tzetzes (*ad* Lyc. 421) both call the seduced mistress Phthia. Homer's ascription of the incident to the town of Eleon in Boeotia has no obvious significance.

The Bellerophon incident is likewise introduced by an erotic episode, the motive here being the well-known one of Potiphar's wife. Again the *novella* yields to a different genre, this time pure *Märchen*. The three hazardous tasks, culminating in the hero's lone slaying of all the bravest warriors lurking in ambush, and the final achievement of the hand of the king's daughter with a dowry of half the realm, all speak the familiar speech of fairy tale. But by now we must be abundantly ready to admit that the maker of oral epic could draw his material whence he liked: he could say, with the motto on the shield, "*Je prends mon bien où je le trouve.*" For us, the immediate interest of the Bellerophon passage must hinge on quite a different issue, since it is one of the few incidents in the Iliad which betrays the date of its composition.

Although greatly incensed at his wife's accusation against Bellerophon, King Proitos

> forebore to slay him; but he sent him unto Lycia and he bestowed on him baneful signs, graving on a folded tablet many life-destroying tokens; these he bade him show to his wife's father, that Bellerophon might perish.

So he fared to Lycia; and the ruler of wide Lycia received him kindly and feasted him for nine days on nine oxen, but on the tenth

> he demanded to see what token he might be bringing from his son-in-law Proitos; and when he had taken in hand his son-in-law's evil token, first he commanded him to slay the terrible Chimaira.

There cannot be much doubt that, in spite of the evasively allusive language, a written message is here intended. A suggestive picture or a group of pictorial symbols might meet the requirements of the narrative but hardly the actual words of the poet. "Graving on a folded tablet" is surely a periphrasis for writing a letter. The story therefore originated in a literate environment; hence it either was imported from some such region as Egypt or

Phoenicia or Assyria, or it was evolved in Ionia after the introduction of writing. It cannot be a stray survival of Mycenaean times, because the epic tradition of heroic illiteracy is clear. Indeed, this must be the very reason why the poet uses such veiled phrases: since writing is for him a modernism, contrary to all epic usage for the Age of Heroes, it must be mentioned with the same indirection as, for example, telescopes by the author of *Paradise Lost* or machinery by a Victorian Romantic. The passage must therefore be of later date than the Ionic contact with the literate East, which (in my partial judgment) would force it well down toward the end of the eighth century. But the Bellerophon episode can be shown to belong even a few decades later, if the following plea will hold.

The Chimaira may be as timeless as most dragons, but the Solymi (against whom the hero is next sent) were historically actual neighbors of the Lycians. When the hero thereafter slays Amazons, this might be taken for a relapse into myth as timeless as the fire-breathing Chimaira. However, later Greek historians identified as Amazons the Cimmerian hordes which overran Asia Minor early in the seventh century. Could the identification be as ancient as Homer? In the course of those terrible raids the Lycians too must have had their troubles in preventing the Cimmerians from breaking into their country. The exact time remains uncertain, since the event could have occurred anywhere in the thirty years between 676 B.C., when the Cimmerians destroyed the power of Phrygia, and 646 B.C., by which time their hordes had retreated east under their leader Tukdamis in a last desperate attempt to reach the rich Assyrian domain, only to have Assurbanipal break their strength just before a new set of northern invaders, the Scythians, finally annihilated them. To identify an assumed Lycian repulse of the Cimmerians with Bellerophon's slaying of the Amazons might seem too preposterous, were it not supported by a second and highly similar reference in the Iliad.

King Priam is talking with Helen on the walls of Troy, and as they survey the Achaean host beneath them on the plain, the old man cries in amazement:

Ah, happy son of Atreus, fortune-born, heaven-favored! many, yea many, are the young men of the Achaeans subject to thee. Once when I went into vine-clad Phrygia, I saw the Phrygian men with their gleaming horses, most numerous encamped by the banks of the Sangarios. For I was mustered as an ally among them on that day when the Amazons came. But even so, they were not as many as are the glancing-eyed Achaeans.

Now, there were no Phrygians in Asia Minor in the Mycenaean period to which Agamemnon's Achaeans supposedly belong; but there were Phrygians later, and perhaps as early as the ninth century these had built up a powerful kingdom on the wreckage of the Hittite empire. This Phrygian kingdom was destroyed by the Cimmerians. We know no details of the catastrophe, save that the Phrygian king Midas killed himself in despair; but it is quite possible, and even probable, that the last stand was made behind the long, curving barrier of the great Phrygian river, the Sangarios. Here all the forces of western Asia Minor would have gathered to stop the terrible archers on horseback, who nonetheless overwhelmed them and rode through them westward to the sea. In the pages of the Greek historian Diodoros, centuries later, these same horsemen are the Amazons. If they were already Amazons for Homer,* the date of Priam's reference must be the year of Midas' downfall, 676 B.C.

It is largely a question of personal judgment—perhaps of prejudice—whether we believe that oral epic poetry made such refer-

* As they already were for fifth-century Greece. At least, the persistent conviction that there were still Amazons living on the banks of the Thermodon near Amisos is too fantastically arbitrary unless it refers to some splintered remnant of the Cimmerian forces settling down after their final encounter with the invading Scythians, much as in Hellenistic times the Gauls were to settle in inland Asia Minor after their defeat by the Pergamenians. Herodotos brings Scythians and Amazons together near the Crimea, the Cimmerian land.

ences to contemporary events under guise of heroic allusion. But before one reaches a verdict, he should consider carefully how frequently just such references in just such guise occur in the Attic dramatists, whose characters discuss current events of Athens and Greece in terms of the distant heroic world. Nor is it inapposite to remark that the Song of Roland has been held by very good modern authorities to have borrowed incidents and details from the (contemporary?) battle of Zalaca in 1086 and Dorylaeum in 1097,* as well as much else in men and manners from the (likewise contemporary?) actualities of the First Crusade, so that the poet might impart more vivid substance to an event three centuries before his time. If the author of the Iliad was an Ionian Greek of the early seventh century, the most impressive and tremendous political event in his lifetime must have been the Cimmerian destruction of the Phrygian empire. Of what else *could* he have been thinking when he made Priam speak of Phrygian armies gathered against the Amazons on the banks of the Sangarios?

The Iliad appears to know Egypt only vaguely as the land of the lordly Ethiopians on Ocean's stream, whither the Olympian gods go to feast and the cranes fly on the approach of winter.† The contrast between this imprecise, half mythological allusion and the detailed knowledge displayed by the Odyssey is a measure

* Cf. *Anonymi Gesta Francorum,* cap. ix.

† It is not necessary to argue that there were really Ethiopians ruling Egypt from 715 to 663 B.C. It would be more pertinent to note that Okeanos, the back-flowing river at the end of the earth, may have had some early identification with the Nile which annually submerged its Delta (to form the original Lake Tritonis?), that the term *Aithiopes* (cf. "redskins"?) is appropriate to the Egyptians, that the identity of Olympian with Egyptian gods was a persistent classical thesis, and that the winter cranes must certainly have flown south. The visits of the Olympians to the lordly Ethiopians became an epic commonplace, which the poet of the Odyssey could employ without any precise geographical connotation. As Egypt and the Delta became actualized for the Greeks, Okeanos and Tritonis and the Ethiopians themselves moved farther into the unexplored. The Ethiopians on Okeanos, who were perhaps only the Egyptians living on either bank, east and west of their great river, could thus become in the Odyssey "the distant Ethiopians, uttermost of men, who are sundered in twain, some dwelling where the Sun-god sinks and others where he rises."

of the difference in date between the two poems. Directly and by name the Iliad mentions Egypt only once, and that single reference is parenthetical, under suspicion of being a later insertion. In spurning Agamemnon's offer of reconciliation in the long and eloquently contemptuous speech which constitutes perhaps the finest oratory in all Greek epic, Achilles cries,

> Not even if he were to give me ten or twenty times as much as he now has . . . or all the wealth assembled at Orchomenos and Thebes,

probably echoing in this final phrase some proverbial expression of the poets. But since Boeotian Thebes, which was the contemporary rival of Orchomenos, was supposed no longer to exist at the time of the Trojan War, our Iliad hastens to explain that by "Thebes" is meant

> the Egyptian, the hundred-gated, where is most treasure stored, whence issue forth through every gate two hundred men with horses and chariots.

This parenthetic elucidation may have been supplied by some later rhapsode. Whoever was responsible for it, such a reference to Egyptian Thebes cannot be older than the seventh century, when the Greeks first resumed contact with the Nile; nor would it have been a very appropriate remark to make after the sack of Egyptian Thebes by the Assyrians in 661. Such a passage dates only itself and not the entire poem in which it occurs; but it is an excellent instance of the historical context through which some sort of chronology for Homer may be established.

In the sixth book, the women of Troy, led by Hecuba, bring a splendid garment to lay on the knees of Athena in her temple atop the town. The passage has been frequently, though not always wisely, discussed. The existence of a closed temple implies a cult statue. The ceremonial of presenting a garment implies that the statue was a rather crude wooden image, or *xoanon,* which, like a modern child's doll, had to be dressed to be presentable. The selection of the garment from a human wardrobe involves a full-sized robe and hence a life-size statue. And unless the phrase be a slip or mere borrowing from stock poetic vocabulary, the presentation by laying on the knees of the goddess implies a statue in a seated pose.

Now, it may pass for established and certain that the practice of cutting life-size nude male human figures out of solid stone was learned by the Greeks from the Egyptians. (None of the marble colossi and life-size "Apollos" which have survived can be dated earlier than the close of the seventh century.) But the practice of making images out of *wood*, and the theme of the throned draped figure, are almost certainly older and seem to have been derived through contact with the civilizations on the extreme eastern shores of the Mediterranean during the so-called "Oriental" phase of Greek culture, which preceded the Egyptian influence by roughly a hundred years. A full-sized wooden statue of a seated woman, whose bodily inadequacies were concealed by actual garments—no doubt with earrings and necklaces of gold added for further adornment,—kept behind the locked doors of a specially built house or shrine, presents us with an archaeological situation readily permissible after the middle of the seventh century, but becoming rapidly less and less probable as we move the date back toward the eighth century, earlier than the final decades of which we may well be permitted to challenge its possibility.

In addition—though it is a huge topic, not casually to be discussed nor briefly to be summarized,—repeated occupation with the famous Catalogue of Ships in the Iliad's second book has convinced me that it demonstrably fails to reflect the politico-geographical conditions of the Late Helladic (Mycenaean) world and that certain of its presuppositions and implications point to the situation in early archaic classical times when Pheidon had extended his rule over Argos, when a league of towns was forming in Boeotia (considerably anterior to the First Sacred War), when after a long lull following the Minoan glory there was a remarkable revival of economic prosperity and regrowth of population in Crete, and when Ionian traders were just beginning to penetrate the Black Sea in order to reëstablish the contact with the Anatolian metalworkers which the Cimmerian invasion had interrupted by cutting the overland caravan connection. This is a highly condensed and completely undemonstrated recapitulation of an intricate theme. If, in spite of that, it be allowed to stand, it adds one more piece of evidence in favor of a date close to 700 B.C.

If we combine these admittedly fragmentary criteria, seeking for a common date to satisfy them, it is a matter of mere inspection to discover that all the requirements will be met only by a short period early in the second quarter of the seventh century. However, this precise span of years cannot be claimed as the proved date of the Iliad's composition, because all of these chronologically critical references are casual, many of them could have been added by the reciting rhapsodes of the seventh century, and none of them occurs in an essential passage or involves extensive portions of the poem. But it is the best that can be done; and it gains greatly in importance by agreeing with the general archaeological cultural setting of the Iliad (which is, in our professional jargon, "Orientalizing"). And it is also to be stressed that, if we overlook the very few "heroic archaisms," there are no other plausible candidates as rival claimants for the title. Nonetheless, there is a slightly variant possibility. If all the scattered contemporary references which I have mentioned are dismissed as rhapsodic accretions from the period of oral transmission before the Iliad was reduced to writing in sixth-century Athens, the cultural environment of the remaining main body of the poem may perfectly well be assigned somewhat earlier, to the latter portion of the eighth century, though hardly to its earlier decades.

To champion a date of comprehensive origin for the Iliad in the tenth or ninth or even the opening of the eighth century betokens—it is a harsh but a just saying!—only ignorance: not ignorance of Homer, but ignorance of the culture of those times.

We emerge with a gap between Odyssey and Iliad of almost certainly half a century. Is this too large for single authorship of both poems? Perhaps not; but there are other considerations to be urged.

The author of the Iliad was a great dramatic artist with remarkable grasp of human character as it can reveal itself in speech. For him, action is often little more than stage business to give his actors their themes and their opportunities to talk. Even the tensest physical conflict is interrupted by dialogue—naïvely, as in the long colloquy between Diomede and Glaukos recounting genealogy in the very press of battle; magnificently, as when Lykaon pleads for his life under Achilles' spear and hears an implacable voice decree his doom; pathetically, as when in the great climax Hector and Achilles speak and reply to each other in no fewer than four pairs of speeches while the final slaying is accomplished. At the comparable point in the Odyssey, when Odysseus

> stripped him of his rags and leaped on to the great threshold with his bow and quiver full of arrows and poured forth all the swift shafts there before his feet,

what an opportunity for an oratorical outburst of hate, scorn, vengeance, and triumph over his doomed adversaries! But he says almost nothing; it is the narrative that speaks.

A young man may be a brilliant storyteller; but the accurate portrayal of human motives and shifting character through the medium of dramatic dialogue is a mature accomplishment, so that even if it lay within a single author's competence to produce narrative like the Odyssey and drama like the Iliad, the temporal sequence is wrong: it is the Odyssey which should have been the youthful work, and not the Iliad.

A vast amount of erudition and patient scholarship has been devoted to the language of the two poems. But this language was a *lingua franca* of the oral poets, and in fifty years it underwent only negligible change. It is not the outer form of the grammatical and metrical vehicle of expression which will betray the unity or duality or plurality of authorship, but the imaginative use to which this identical language has been put, the preferences and antipathies which, unknown to the poets themselves, underlie all creative literary activity.*

To the poet of the Iliad dogs are unclean scavengers—just as to Shakespeare they were all curs. The Iliad contains no kindly or even halfway sympathetic word for their breed. But the poet of the Odyssey is a friend and lover of the race of dogs: his was the moving anecdote of old Argos dying with joy at sound of his returning master's voice; in addition, we can discover that he knew about feeding dogs with tidbits from the table and delighted to take them on walks, that he did not resent a whelping bitch's warning growl or her threat to attack any stranger approaching her puppies; and he had seen with pity an unwanted litter disposed of, not as we do by drowning, but by dashing the heads against the stony ground, and when he came to describe the cannibal Cyclops seizing Odysseus' comrades to devour them, this was the picture that flashed across his mind. He makes even the brutal ogre suddenly soften as he fondles and addresses the old ram which used to lead the flock. But the poet of the Iliad is not attracted to animals. He has a "phobia" about lions—which do not always behave very much like lions, but like fierce Greek shepherd dogs that have turned against their master and started killing his herds. The poet of the Odyssey entertains no such terrors. Although the Iliad must have made lions a literary commonplace, there are only half a dozen allusions to them in the

* Such a method of analysis has been elaborated and ably advocated for the Elizabethan dramatists by Caroline Spurgeon in her *Shakespeare's Imagery*. It should be susceptible of application to Greek epic.

Odyssey; and in one of these, instead of dwelling fearfully on the ferocity of the beast, the poet shows so much animal sympathy that it is the lion's own terror when surrounded by hunters which comes uppermost. In exchange, the poet of the Iliad thinks fondly and gently of children, on which the poet of the Odyssey never wastes an approving word. Radiance, glitter, and glimmer; the flashing of fire on earth and the shining of stars in heaven; storm, mist, cloud, and lightning: these are unfailing sources for the Iliad's imagery and are ever at the back of the author's mind. In none of these (save for trite commonplaces such as belong to everyone, or occasional echoes and borrowings for which the reciting rhapsodes may equally well be held accountable) does the poet of the Odyssey follow. For him a storm is a storm—a blind night of pouring rain and wind from the sea—rather than a source of imagery. He can describe a tempest; but he does not think in terms of it for his poetic fancies.

By pursuing analyses such as these, seeking not differences of syntax or grammatical usage or paradigms of inflection, but for the brain and heart of the artist behind them, I have convinced myself (and hope on due occasion to convince others) that—with proper allowance made for the inevitable changes and accretions due to oral repetition and transmission—the Iliad which we know was essentially the work of a single author, and our Odyssey was the work of a single author; but these two authors could not possibly have been one and the same.

How fundamentally different the two great poems are must also become apparent from our assay of fact, fable, and fiction in their content. An underlying and all-pervasive folk tale has assured to the Odyssey a narrative tone through all fictional adornment and epic development; while for the Iliad the balance tilts in quite an opposite direction. Here the basic component is not folk tale but heroic saga, oral tradition of distant actual event. Saga too, like folk tale, hangs on incident, but not on incident in the long sequences of a patterned plot. To saga belong the willful accidents attendant on human character; around its unforgotten heroes cluster dramatic act and tragic circumstance. Shifting adventure and external vicissitude give place to more centralized personal emotion, more widely human relationships.

In both poems, fiction has proved to be the prime component. This was so because the historic actualities of saga had become as thin and vague through lapse of time as the *Märchen* world of folk tale was remote in place and alien in setting. Thus the poet himself had most to contribute if he would make either poem real, persuasive, and appealing. Each poem, so largely fashioned out of a different pair of oral epic's elements, had little interest left for the missing third component: the folk-tale epic of the Odyssey contained but little saga, and the heroic saga epic of the Iliad gave folk tale only a precarious and unessential place. In neither poem should we ask for factual record or truthful history. Both—it seems strange that this still needs again and again to be discovered!—are primarily works of literary art. Neither belongs to prehistory, not to Mycenaean times nor yet to the poverty-stricken centuries which immediately succeeded: both belong to Greece, classic Greece, which produced so soon after them Sappho and Aeschylos and Plato.

POSTSCRIPT: 1946

A YEAR has passed since the preceding lectures were delivered. They have been printed exactly as they were composed, although not quite as they were orally presented, since not all of their content could be fitted into the straitened hour of the academic tradition. A small amount of supplementary material appears as footnotes; but no attempt has been made to support the text by expanding its arguments or enumerating its documentary sources. Even to establish a bibliography for its intricate network of affiliated topics would have overwhelmed the individual lectures. As everyone knows, the literature of the Homeric Question is enormous and not always profitable: to have further expanded it with book and journal references to related matters of folklore, oral epic, and religious and miscellaneous classical antiquities would have increased the bulk by at least as much again. The Sather Lectures are intended for a general public of intelligent, sympathetically interested, but not necessarily highly specialized listeners. Thus, even in printed form, they may still claim to be lectures rather than overblown articles from professional journals, and serve their end most fitly by remaining free of the elaborate dissections of the seminar and the heavier trappings of erudition, which—to mix the metaphor quite irremediably—are only too often the cheap coin of scholarship.

The dangers in discoursing easily on difficult matters and offering concise conclusions from inevident evidence are obvious. Yet to do anything else would have been to change the whole character of the book. Perhaps those who have already penetrated the various disciplines will recognize allusions, appreciate connotations, and accept for what they are the choices and decisions which had to be made if anything intelligible and coherent was to be presented.

When I pause to consider how preposterous the Bearson and

other ursine connections of Odysseus will appear to the classicist who has spent a satisfactory lifetime without them, I cannot be too thankful that, at any rate, Beowulf students have already been through all this—even though I am aware that the bimillennial superiority of the Hellenist will leave him loath to admit that any illumination won by his more barbarous colleagues from northern lands in postclassical times can bring him enlightenment. Yet it is just here that the chief contribution of these lectures may hope to lodge. The Mediterranean archaeologists, with their truly marvelous anacalypsis of the preclassical Cretan and Mycenaean (or, as they prefer to term them, Minoan and Helladic) cultures, have dazzled the Homericists and misled them into thinking that this new light on the Aegean world of the second millennium B.C. was shining also for their Homeric studies. But poetry inherits, cherishes, and re-utilizes more out of its own medium of expression than it assimilates from the material and artistic horizons of the past; and the poetical speech of the Greeks was European, not Aegean. In order to explore the background and ancestry of Homeric epic we must travel north, not east or south.

To accept such a thesis—and I do not see how its acceptance can rightly be refused—may seem to doom us to the darkness of perpetual ignorance, because the period and the civilization to which we are appealing (the Danubian and North European prehistoric epoch) is infinitely less explored and less explorable than prehistoric Greece. Everything hinges on the uncertain possibility that there may be survivals from this remote inaccessible past amid other European nations than the Greeks, detectable in more recent than classical times. Any basic identity between the Danish–Early English Beowulf and the Aeolic-Ionic Odyssey is therefore crucial. Far from apologizing for the time and space which was devoted to it, I should probably have insisted even more strongly upon it.

King Hrothgar's ale hall and the Cyclops' cave heavily stocked with food, to which the Greeks add their wine for potent drink, should not be idly ingenious parallels. Hrothgar is not using his ale hall, allegedly through terror at the monster's depredations, but fundamentally (I suppose) because the folktale demands that the place of trial should be an empty house in full working order. The Odyssean version, where this is emphasized, is therefore accurate and the parallel pertinent. In both poems, the monster breaks suddenly upon the scene after the visitors are comfortably installed. The *μασχαλισμός* of Grendel (if that is what it is) and the blinding of Polyphemos are both intelligible as attempts to render harmless a demon which cannot be directly destroyed. The pursuit into the underworld (delayed in the Odyssey by the catenization of the episodes) is told in northern legend as a swimmer's exploit down a maelstrom or plunging water. In Icelandic saga, Grettir dives under the waterfall; in Beowulf, the hero in full armor swims deep down through churning waters where "tossing spray mounts dark to heaven." The Odyssey may preserve some of this same tradition:

> soon I descried smoke and a great surf and heard the sea bellowing,

and a little later there is Charybdis, above which

> the spray aloft fell atop of either cliff.

The dismal mere in Beowulf, "where trees firm-rooted o'ershroud the wave with shadowing gloom," is well matched by the Odyssey with

> the roots of the fig-tree spread far below, and aloft out of reach its huge branches hung, overshadowing Charybdis.

I am persuaded that here again the parallel is sound; but I cannot for a moment convince myself that any direct influence percolated from the Odyssey to the poet of Beowulf. He and Homer must be independently tapping a common and widespread narrative source. It would be gratuitous to insist on discovering the precise form in which this narrative reached either of them.

In ascribing the transmission of this and related bear-cult legends in Greece to a Thracian infiltration of Phokis and northwestern Boeotia, I may have lacked a proper courage. Were it not for the acknowledged Thracian associations of Daulis, Trophonios, and the Abantes, it would perhaps have been better to deny the need for any such bridge between the Danubian Getai of Herodotos and the Phthian or Phokian mythologic tradition of classic times. If an archaeologist, in examining the "structural style of the Getic mountain fortresses" and discovering "many archaic elements which point to the closest of relations with the [Hellenic] South," can wonder whether such similarities may be due not to immediate contact between Gete and Greek but to "survivals of the common Central European inheritance of the second millennium B.C. when the Greeks themselves inhabited these Danubian countries,"* why should not the literary student be entitled to claim a like privilege and postulate equally persistent immaterial survivals such as myths and folk tales and cult superstitions, all of which would have clung with extreme tenacity to the vehicle of that European language which the Aeolic Greeks brought with them out of the Danubian region into Thessaly and Boeotia?

In marshaling the elusive evidence for bear-cult survivals amid the Aeolid stories of Greek legend I have included everything that could be found, without venturing to evaluate between the convincing and the improbable. To ask the listener or the reader to pass judgment here is perhaps to prejudice his verdict. Yet how is one, whether scholar or layman, to reach a sound and acceptable decision? Melikertes is much more likely to be the "honey-eater" than the unintelligible *"Honigschneider"* acclaimed by the Wilamowitzan School (if only because no one spends his time cutting

* V. Parvan, *Dacia* (Cambridge, 1928), p. 102.

honey); but if he *is* the honey-eater, then certainly he is the bear. He and his mother Ino are in the water together, where perhaps they both drown; yet as Palaimon and Leukothea they survive. In the Odyssey Ino, the same Ino,

> the fair-ankled daughter of Kadmos, even Leukothea
> who once was a speaking mortal but now in the salty deep
> by the gods' grace has been accorded honor,

comes up out of the sea and sits like a sea gull on Odysseus' raft. When he is hurled into the water, her assistance preserves him from drowning. Is her entirely unexpected and quite unnecessary presence here a survival by association from the Melikertes story because Odysseus the prodigious swimmer is the Bearson? We have no scholarly method for dealing with such imponderabilia.

Something more might have been made of the intriguing parallel—relegated to a footnote—between the second part of Beowulf and the Telegony sequel to the Odyssey, which is admittedly very puzzling and at first sight completely inexplicable. Students of the Early English epic have always been at a loss to explain the complete absence of coherence or continuity between Beowulf's major exploit against Grendel and the concluding episode, with the fifty years of intervening rule dismissed in twelve verses without mention of the slightest event until

> a fire-drake flying in darkness of night
> on the upland heather guarded a hoard,
> a stone barrow lofty: under it lay
> a path concealed from the sight of men.
> There a thief broke in on the heathen treasure,
> laid hand on a flagon all fretted with gold,
> as the dragon discovered.*

Beowulf, accompanied by only one faithful companion, battles the dragon and slays it at price of his own life. With the hero's funeral and the erection of a great memorial barrow close to the sea,

* The quotation is from Kennedy's translation.

broad and high on the brow of the cliff,
seen from afar by seafaring men,

the epic ends.

The Odysseus legend displays a similar discontinuity, with a cleavage into two wholly unrelated series of events. Homer recounts only the first of these and terminates (like the first part of Beowulf) with the triumphant homecoming of the hero to his native land and his assumption of kingly title and power. But there must have been already current the sequel which appears sketchily as an "advance notice" in Teiresias' picturesque prophecy to Odysseus in the underworld. In terms of the Odyssey's own plot this is gratuitous, intrusive, and completely without point; and yet it is the only discoverable climax or purpose in the underworld adventure. Although it is lamely allowed to drop by the poet, who cannot use it in his poem, it is to reappear as the initial impulse which sets the Telegony in motion: *ἔπειτα εἰς Ἰθάκην καταπλεύσας τὰς ὑπὸ Τειρεσίου ῥηθείσας τελεῖ θυσίας*, says the epitome by Proklos. How death at the last overtook the hero who had worsted death and escaped unscathed from death's shadowy kingdom—this must be the dominant theme demanding a sequel to the Bearson adventure. Since it justifies the otherwise objectionable dichotomy of the Beowulf epic and links the Telegony to the Odyssey, I must again urge that so basic an observation is not likely to depend on a merely chance resemblance.

The parallel runs even closer (although by becoming still more mysterious it can hardly become any more convincing!) when it is further observed that the second part of Beowulf and the Telegony of Eugammon both open with the description of a remarkable precious cup, the "flagon all fretted with gold," the loss of which rouses the old dragon in the English poem, and the mixing bowl adorned with the legend of Trophonios and Agamedes, which seems such a pointless prelude to the lost Greek poem. Has it some hidden pertinence? Is Trophonios the same Trophonios who had the oracular den above Lebadeia? And if so, is he, like his "over-wily" double, who steals the golden treasure a little at a time, undetected, by breaking into the sealed storeroom, a typically Greek humanization of the bear who keeps robbing the bees' golden hive until he is trapped by the enraged owner? in which event the story would naturally be assimilated to the Bear-son tales? One would suppose not. Yet it is worth reflecting that, instead of bewitching men into animals as northern fairy tale does with its hero becoming frog or swan or fourfoot beast, the Greek always treated animals as though they were men (whence the inveterate human psychology of Aesop's fables, in many of which, if we were not expressly informed that the characters are supposed to be fox or wolf or lion, we should have every justification for insisting that they were human beings and quite normal citizens in a Greek community). Would not this be the selfsame metempsychosis which transformed Salmoxis the bear into Salmoxis the slave of Pythagoras? On the contrary side, the argument recently in favor, whereby the tale of Trophonios and Agamedes is brought to Greece out of Egypt by way of Eugammon's home town of Cyrene and is identified in its proper Egyptian dress in Herodotos' diverting story of Rhampsinitos and the Thief—all this is unconvincing, because there are un-Egyptian traits in the Rhampsinitos story (such as the beards on the king's guardsmen) and an Ionian twist to the clever tricks and the scurrilous humor, which make me think that Herodotos heard the story from his fellow countrymen in Naukratis and that these had brought it to Egypt with them out of their homeland. No one in discussing the tale seems to lay any emphasis on its significant close:

And they say that after these happenings the king descended alive into what the Greeks call Hades, and there he threw dice with Demeter, sometimes winning and sometimes losing, and came back again to the upperworld with a golden napkin as her gift. They also said that the Egyptians instituted a festival in commemoration of Rhampsinitos' descent and return. Now, I myself saw them celebrating this in my own day; but I cannot say whether this was indeed the reason for that festival.

There follows a brief account of a newly woven garment carried by a blindfold priest whom two wolves reputedly conduct five miles, leading him to a sanctuary of "Demeter" and back again to town.

Herodotos was no doubt correct in his suspicion that the Egyptian rite and festival which he witnessed were not founded on any Rhampsinitan descent into the underworld. Are we in turn equally correct in our suspicion that, whether it was the king or the thief who rolled dice with Death and escaped from deadman's land, the attachment of this characteristic Bearson adventure to the tale of the Master Thief is as significant as the Telegony's attachment of the tale of the Master Thief to the life history of the Bearson?

There is another struggle with the death demon and a triumphant return from the realm of the departed, for which there was not time or space in the crowded galley of my seventh lecture. The heroic discomfiture of Death, the Devourer, the Intruder on the happy feast of life, which I have taken to be the primal reference in Beowulf's wrestling with Grendel and Odysseus' ordeal with Polyphemos, likewise inspires the plot of Euripides' romantic and ever-popular play *Alkestis*. Herakles' unsensitive and gluttonous behavior may well be part of the dramatic poet's deliberate intention; but I doubt whether it originated with him or yet in any tradition of satyr play or Phlyakan farce, so much as in the inevitable banquet hall of the folk tale. Death has entered the king's palace and dragged away a victim. The king himself is helpless to cope with his calamity, when a wandering stranger hero arrives from afar and takes up his watch in the hall of feasting and drinking, of which he partakes. It is here that he should have wrestled with the Intruder; but since he must also bring back the captive princess from the underworld, he follows the trail of the demon to Alkestis' tomb and there throws him in a bout. The story is Thessalian and Aeolid (Alkestis being a descendant of Salmoneus and Kretheus). Herakles' assumption of the Bearson role is somewhat startling. Yet Herakles (as the ancients perceived) is a composite figure; and the Theban child of a god's violence, with a colorless adoptive mortal father, preternaturally strong of arm, descending into the underworld and reëmerging (if we may trust Euripides' *Herakles Mainomenos*) after all but his nearest relatives believed him dead, and achieving ultimately (if we may accept Homer) a somewhat unstable immortality, with his revivified body among the everliving Olympians, but his swarthy *eidolon* among the dead—may have been assimilating traits from the ubiquitous folk tale to which these lectures were so attentive.

The legend of Kephalos and Prokris may likewise have deserved more exploitation than a footnote gave, because it may really bear on the pre-Homeric source of Penelope's character. If there was a familiar story pattern in which the wife failed to recognize her own husband and was wooed and won by him before he revealed his true identity, this might have been responsible for Odysseus' heartlessness toward Penelope, whom he continues to keep in the dark and exclude from his confidence long after he has revealed himself to Telemachos and been discovered by Eurykleia. And it would also explain the curious turn of the plot (which Homer recognizes but glosses over) in which Odysseus, while still disguised as a beggar, technically wins Penelope for his bride by meeting the conditions which she herself set to her suitors:

> "Whoso shall most easily string the bow in his hands and shoot through all twelve axes, with him will I go and foresake this house."

The situation is brushed aside by Penelope, who anticipates the outcome by demanding of the suitors,

"Do you imagine that if yonder stranger strings the great bow of Odysseus in the pride of his might and the strength of his arm, he will lead me home to make me his wife?! He has no such hope in his heart; so fret not yourself on that account."

I may therefore have been wrong in taking the poet's insistent flattering contrast of the faithful Penelope to the unfaithful Klytaimnestra as quite so primary in the creation of her character.

If it belongs to the story pattern that the wife shall be unable to recognize her husband, it may also be part of the story that the old father shall not recognize his son—which may rescue the chief incident of the Odyssey's closing book from the oft-repeated charge of being a later rhapsode's supplement. As for the final close, which also has found small favor with modern critics, my anachronistic comparisons of the Iliad's structure to that of Attic tragedy might have for Odyssean corollary the suggestion that the final reconciliation by the arbitrary device of a *deus ex machina* with its ensuing peaceful and permanent settlement under divine sanction may have appealed as much to a Homeric as to a later Euripidean audience, being a proper Greek way to end a heroic narrative of violence. In short, the poem never did stop at ψ 296; and I dare say that the ancient critics Aristophanes and Aristarchos did not mean anything more by their supposed stricture than that the central theme of the story had reached its logical conclusion when Odysseus and Penelope were at last reunited.

This book has no Preface. Had it had one, its prime function would have been the traditional expression of grateful satisfactions. In particular, it would have given me opportunity to record the kindly hospitality of Berkeley, the unwaveringly tolerant helpfulness of the Committee on the Sather Lectures and the no less tolerant helpfulness of the experienced Editor of the University of California Press. But this most pleasant of obligations can equally well be discharged in a postscript and end, rather than initiate, a book which has been a stimulation to write, a diversion to read in public, and a satisfaction to see so promptly in print.

INDEX